IMAGES
of America

HEGEWISCH

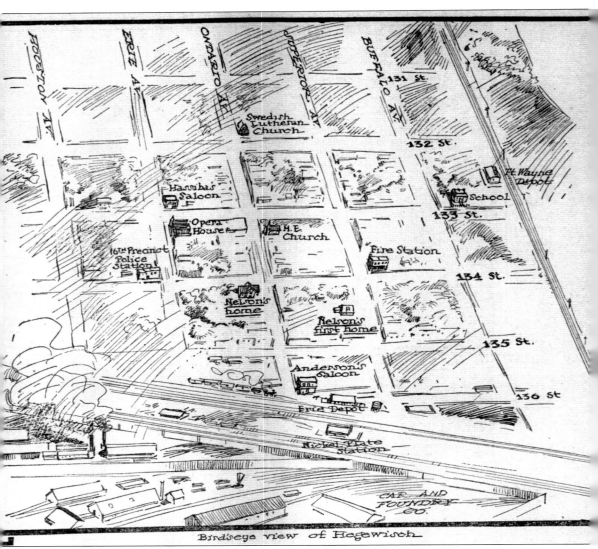

Part of an *Inter Ocean* newspaper article, this quirky map of Hegewisch commemorated Oscar Battling Nelson's lightweight boxing championship and the neighborhood of Hegewisch in 1905. Shown are both of the Nelson family's houses, the Opera House, three train stations, two saloons, a fire station, and a police station. Housed in a former saloon, the police station was short-lived and never replaced. (Southeast Chicago Historical Museum.)

ON THE COVER: This railroad station served the South Chicago & Southern Railroad, which later became part of the Chicago, Pittsburgh & Fort Wayne line. Besides having a passenger waiting area, there was a telegraph office and a small freight depot. Water tanks for locomotives were located north of the station. For a while, Hegewisch had two other passenger stations for the Nickel Plate and the Chicago & Western Indiana (CWI) Railroads, respectively. (Southeast Chicago Historical Museum.)

IMAGES
of America

HEGEWISCH

Cynthia L. Ogorek

ARCADIA
PUBLISHING

Published by Arcadia Publishing
Charleston, South Carolina

Printed in the United States of America

Library of Congress Control Number: 2023945829

For all general information, please contact Arcadia Publishing:
Telephone 843-853-2070
Fax 843-853-0044
E-mail sales@arcadiapublishing.com

Visit us on the Internet at www.arcadiapublishing.com

To my parents, Lucie Pavich, who was raised in Hegewisch, and Walter Ogorek, born and raised in Arizona. They were the inspiration for this book.

CONTENTS

ACKNOWLEDGMENTS

Thank you to Champaign County (Ohio) Historical Society and Scott D. Trostel. In Alabama, thanks to the Decatur Public Library, Alabama Room; the Morgan County Archives; and the Public Library of Anniston and Calhoun County.

My aunts and uncles were not aware decades ago that I was listening when they played "Who Was She From Home?" Over the cake and coffee, someone would say the name of a Hegewisch woman. There would be some murmuring, then someone would ask, "Who was she from home?" With the maiden name, they quoted the genealogy and added personal anecdotes until the next name came up and the game restarted. I learned a lot about Hegewisch this way.

At the Southeast Chicago Historical Society Museum, special thanks to Rod Sellers, the society's longtime volunteer archivist; to Joann Podkul; Carolyn Mulac; Karen Brozynski; and Anthony Margis.

I wish to thank the staffs of the University of California, Berkeley; New York Public Library; Chicago Public Library; and the South Suburban Genealogical and Historical Society.

Mike Aniol of Aniol's Tru Value Hardware was generous with his great collection of photographs. If Aniol's was the informal photograph archive, then the South Shore Inn owned by Dean and Lisa Ubik was the informal Hegewisch museum. Their tavern itself is a time capsule crammed with photographs and framed maps of long-ago Hegewisch.

Thank you to my friend and local historian Ruth Mores for sharing her Ancestry.com expertise; to Amanda Aguilera of the Hammond Public Library's Local History Room; to Barry Henderson, Queens University-Belfast; and to Eddie Hegewisch for information regarding his great-great-uncle Adolf Hegewisch. Thank you to Bill Molony, my go-to guy for Chicago's railroad history. Michael Boos, producer of "Calumet Revisited," gave me an opportunity to try out my material in front of a live audience. Tom Shepherd's tours of wetlands and landfills schooled me in the protests of the 1970s and 1980s. And much appreciation goes to fellow writer and editor Robert Runyard, who assisted with last minute photograph and information searches and the writing of the text.

Images from the Southeast Chicago Historical Museum are noted by SCHM.

INTRODUCTION

The year is 1905. A reporter gets off the train at the CWI station and crosses the street to Anderson's Saloon. He has come to Hegewisch to find out about the town and the man: the man being Oscar "Battling" Nelson, soon to be crowned the world's lightweight boxing champion.

At Anderson's he gets directions to the Nelson house, and he walks through Hegewisch, noting how quiet it is. The streets are not paved. There is water in ditches. Willow trees predominate. He had already noticed as suburban Chicago was left behind, that the landscape had turned to prairie. Now he found himself in what appeared to be a country town.

After he interviewed Nelson's family, he continued strolling and found himself at the police station on Baltimore Avenue near 134th Street. The officer told him that he had just received a new ledger in which to record arrests. By his reckoning, it would take until 5905 to fill it in as Hegewisch had no crime.

Then he interviewed E.M. Skinner, a grocer. Skinner acknowledged the common feeling in Hegewisch that "the city has never done anything for our streets and it doesn't make any difference what administration is in, we don't cast enough votes to make it an object to the city to do anything to fix up the town. The people here are prosperous, but we can't get anything done, and that is the reason the town seems to be in such bad shape. It is not our fault."

Hegewisch had been founded a little over 20 years earlier by the Hegewisch Land Company as an adjunct to the United States Rolling Stock Company. The president of the latter company, Adolf Hegewisch, acted as trustee for the land syndicate, and seemed to be available to the people who came there to live and work. In the 1930s, John Harris recalled that Adolf Hegewisch presided over a meeting of residents regarding the need for a schoolhouse. He was also instrumental in siting the railroad station and the Opera House, assisting with building churches, and acquiring a fire engine from the Village of Hyde Park.

But the story of Hegewisch started in New York state in the 1860s with the merger of three railroads that became the Atlantic & Great Western Railway Company (A&GW). The A&GW was foreclosed in 1871, then sold to William Butler Duncan, Allen G. Thurman, and Gen. George B. McClellan. The latter was also president of the United States Rolling Stock Company (USRSC), a New York firm manufacturing, selling, and leasing locomotives and freight cars. USRSC's chief customers were the Erie and the A&GW railroads.

Around the time of the Panic of 1873, McClellan resigned and James B. Hodgskin took over as president. His vice president was William H. Guion, with Adolf Hegewisch as treasurer and secretary. USRSC's home office was in New York City, but its plant was located in Urbana, Ohio, at the junction of the Erie; the Pittsburg, Cleveland, Chicago & St. Louis; and the Cleveland, Cincinnati, Chicago & St. Louis Railroads.

Remarkably, while other companies in 1873 were declaring bankruptcy in droves, USRSC experienced phenomenal growth because it was able to produce cars for the railroads, which in the panic had to eliminate their own car factories. With confidence in its future, USRSC looked to expand its operations to Chicago, an even bigger railroad hub.

In Chicago, Hodgskin easily cut a deal for property on the South Branch of the Chicago River. A small article in the *Chicago Tribune* of October 14, 1876, described it as 13-plus acres with docks, buildings, machinery, and tools. Shortly after this, Hodgskin resigned for health reasons, and Adolf Hegewisch became president.

By 1882, USRSC was considered to be the largest car builder in the United States. In the previous year, the mechanical department had spent $1,294,979 to construct 1,377 boxcars and 1,098 flatcars, which consumed 13 million feet of lumber, 7,000 tons of metal fittings, and 17,710 car wheels. Now it ventured beyond manufacturing and leasing to finance the purchase of its own rolling stock. It was called the "car trust" plan. Then it announced the purchase of land in the Calumet Region, specifically the southeast corner of Hyde Park Township.

Since the end of the Civil War "large manufacturing interests" had been exploring the Calumet Region for likely building sites because the area offered cheap land with access to water and rail transportation without the taxes of Chicago. The Calumet and Chicago Canal and Dock Company controlled 5,000 acres of land along the Calumet River, which it had begun advertising for sale in 1874, promising low prices, low taxes, and low construction costs. All very attractive to USRSC.

A plat of the proposed factory showed a wood-working mill, car-erecting shops, paint shops and kilns, along with engine and boiler houses, a car-truck shop, storehouse, assorted metal-working shops, locomotive and car repair shops, a lumberyard, and rail sidings capable of storing 1,000 cars. By December 1883, tracks had been laid. Soon the main shops were enclosed and the factory engines were running, but there was no place for workers to live.

So, nine investors set up the Hegewisch Land Company and bought several hundred acres north of the plant. Adolf Hegewisch made it clear that this would not be another Pullman, where the company and its president controlled the very lifestyle of the town's inhabitants.

Three years later, in December 1887, USRSC built two more car plants: one in Anniston, Alabama, and another at Decatur, Alabama. In January 1889, the monthly payroll for the 725 Anniston employees alone was $25,000. That year, too, Hegewisch became part of the city of Chicago in an annexation move that included all the collar townships around the city. Now instead of dealing with Adolf Hegewisch, Hegewisch people dealt with an alderman who had other interests besides Hegewisch's needs and, bottom line, needed votes.

Unlike its neighbors to the north, Hegewisch, located in the Wolf Lake basin, was built on peat deposits overlain by sand with some areas of standing water, just as the reporter had noticed.

In its natural state, the area was dominated by Lake Calumet, Hyde Lake, and Wolf Lake, all of which were surrounded by marshes. Before USRSC came along, the Hegewisch area was often called a "hunter's paradise."

The water also held a fascination for industrial entrepreneurs. Water meant transportation of goods, but water could also be made into land by filling it. USRSC was the first to make such changes when it dredged the river to make a slip, using the spoils to shore up its building site. Later came other industrial concerns, settling north of Hegewisch, which filled in parts of Wolf Lake and the entire Hyde Lake, while depositing their toxic wastes in the river, the lakes, and the marshes. In the 1890s, an era of great public works began with the construction of the Chicago Sanitary and Ship Canal, leading to the creation of the Lakes-to-Gulf Waterway involving the Calumet River on Hegewisch's west side.

The 1890s also brought another financial panic. USRSC's car trust plan hit a snag in November 1890 when Baring Brothers of London, the major holder of the company's capital stock and bonds, failed. USRSC went into receivership, and the court appointed Adolf Hegewisch as receiver, ordering him to continue operations at all of the plants.

In Hegewisch, the labor force was reduced from 2,500 to 500, while Adolf Hegewisch hoped that the continued operation of the Anniston factory would salvage the entire company. His efforts there proved futile. The London stockholders wanted to force a foreclosure.

Over the next two years, lawyers, investors, bondholders, and creditors wrangled over the disposition of the company's assets. On June 1, 1891, a committee of stockholders created a reorganization plan that would benefit all but the unsecured creditors. William Brander, a London stockholder and a member of the Reorganization Committee, petitioned for foreclosure of the mortgages and sale of all the properties.

The following month, the court heard a claim that Adolph Hegewisch, as receiver, had mismanaged the business, incurred frivolous expenses, and had overdrawn his salary. Hegewisch denied the charges in court in January, adding that when the books for 1891 were closed, they would show "but little loss." He was further accused of voluntarily being party to a scheme perpetrated by the Reorganization Committee to sell out at a profit. In February, he was replaced as receiver by William Lane.

Then a suit was filed against William Brander, claiming that he had sued for foreclosure because that would favor the Reorganization Committee. The Reorganization Committee, meanwhile, tried to have USRSC's assets turned over to Lane and, by April 1892, managed to reorganize USRSC under the name United States Car Company (US Car).

That summer, the properties at Hegewisch and Anniston were leased to US Car of New Jersey. G.W. Ristine, the new manager, said Hegewisch was in pretty bad shape, but he hoped to get work underway in October.

The Hegewisch plant was sold at auction on May 22, 1893, to the Reorganization Committee, which resumed operations under the name of US Car. In 1897, US Car was foreclosed and reorganized as Illinois Car. By the time the *Inter Ocean* reporter toured Hegewisch, the property had been leased by Western Steel Car and Foundry, which bought the concern in 1912.

In the midst of this turmoil, Hegewisch remained a small, quiet town, which since Chicago had taken over, had a new public school, a flourishing business district, and a public park with a gate and a fence. "Bat" Nelson made his home there and owned a considerable amount of property.

In 1908, the Chicago South Shore & South Bend interurban added a stop in Hegewisch to its schedule between South Bend, Indiana, and Chicago. Nine years later, the Chicago streetcar line reached Hegewisch with its terminal at the South Shore station on Brainard Avenue. Now, local people could commute to General Chemical, north of town, as well as the new Republic Steel plant on the other side of Hyde Lake.

The Cal-Sag Channel, the other part of the Chicago Sanitary District's plan to reverse the flow of polluted water away from Lake Michigan, opened in 1922. After World War I, the Ford Motor Company opened its plant on Torrence Avenue, and Hegewisch experienced a boom in housing and commercial development in the area around 130th Street and Torrence Avenue. In 1926, Western Steel was folded into the Pressed Steel Car Company (PSC) and assumed that name locally.

During the years of the Great Depression, some Hegewisch people were hard-hit, losing jobs or being employed only part-time. Others managed to open businesses on Baltimore Avenue and elsewhere. In 1936, "Doc" Simborg began publishing the *Hegewisch News Weekly*. In 1932, the park district built a field house at Mann Park, 25 years after the park had been designated.

As the Depression weakened, public works projects on the Calumet River continued with the realignment of the channel westward in preparation to receive a lock and dam structure. The year 1939 saw a proposal to build a Lake Calumet Airport. In order to do this, the city would have to fill in 300 acres on its north end with refuse. By 1941, the airport project was dead, but the landfill continued.

Then came World War II. Hegewisch had its own Office of Civil Defense. PSC refitted its long-shuttered plant to produce Sherman tanks.

After the war, PSC faced the facts: the railroad industry was a feast-or-famine situation. The best means to profitability was diversification. All its car manufacturing went to a plant in Mount Vernon, Illinois, while at Hegewisch, it retooled the factory to produce household appliances.

The *Hegewisch News* changed hands. The baby boom increased population. There were now three elementary schools, and the Chicago Public Library (CPL) was still using the "library stores" system in Hegewisch until it finally agreed in 1958 to send a bookmobile to town once a week.

One solution to the postwar housing shortage was a trailer park on the south shore of Wolf Lake. This was followed by a new subdivision west of it and north of 133rd Street. Then, a subdivision called Avalon Trails sprang up north of 130th Street and east of Torrence Avenue.

Work on the Lakes-to-Gulf Waterway resumed, and by the mid-1950s, the St. Lawrence Seaway had opened the door to oceangoing craft at Lake Calumet Harbor. Shortly thereafter, the O'Brien Lock and Dam on the Calumet River was functional, and Hegewisch found itself at the heart of an inland transportation corridor. The waterway combined with the Calumet Expressway, connected Hegewisch with many other freeways and toll roads throughout the Chicago area.

But progress and prosperity brought worries about pollution from the steel mills at East Side, South Deering, and South Chicago to the north and from smaller but polluting industries that were lining Lake Calumet and the west bank of the Calumet River. The Southeast Sportsmen's Club moved its headquarters to the shores of Wolf Lake in Hegewisch in the mid-1950s, making it known that one of its purposes was to protect Wolf Lake. The club joined the Hegewisch chamber of commerce to oppose the extension of 130th Street from Lake Calumet Harbor to Indiana via Wolf Lake.

The end of an era arrived in 1956 when PSC, now known as US Industries, sold its property to US Steel, which created a block of warehouses there for its steel products. The entrance to the property also changed from the Brandon-Brainard factory gate to a driveway on Torrence Avenue. The traditional hub of Hegewisch activity as well as railcar production was no more.

After years of "begging," Hegewisch convinced the CPL in 1960 that it was worthy of a proper library, now housed in a former hardware store on Brandon Avenue where students and adults could access a permanent collection of books five or six days a week. The same year, the park district granted the neighborhood a swimming pool at Mann Park, some 28 years after the field house was built and 53 years after the park had been opened.

Although vandalism had people on edge in the 1960s, Hegewisch had no police station because crime statistics showed in black and white that there was "no crime" here. It was still a quiet, isolated, small-town kind of community. In the spirit of taking care of its own, Avalon Trails subdivision formed the Avalon Trails Improvement Association (ATIA), which produced a monthly newsletter that focused on neighborhood events and the big issues in Hegewisch such as the extension of 130th Street; the deplorable state of 130th Street as it was; the nuisance of the intersection of 130th Street with Brainard Avenue, Torrence Avenue, and the CWI railroad tracks; and the railroad embankment that threatened to cut off the northwest side of the neighborhood.

When the editor and publisher of the *Hegewisch News* died in 1971, his wife took over and found herself leading the opposition to turning Hegewisch into Chicago's "city dump." Landfills and pollution became the watchwords of the 1970s and 1980s. In the midst of this controversy, the ATIA's Library Committee spent years convincing the Library Board to build a proper library for Hegewisch. Its victory euphoria lasted two months until the city proposed to obliterate Hegewisch altogether in pursuing a relatively cheap way to contain the factory pollution north of town and create jobs for people who would no longer live there: this was to be the Lake Calumet Airport.

Landfill protesters reorganized themselves as "Third Airport" protesters. In the end, it became a question of land use—how to control landfills and how to save an important expanse of wetlands on the southeast side of Chicago. From this 20-year conflict, two long-lived organizations emerged: the Southeast Environmental Task Force and the Calumet Ecological Park Association.

Speaking into tape recorders in later years, people who grew up in Hegewisch recalled how much fun they had had in the prairies and along the shores of Wolf Lake with their isolation and peacefulness making it a "children's paradise."

Their oral histories also documented the social life of the town and how even in the 1990s and early 2000s, they still considered Hegewisch to be a town rather than just another Chicago neighborhood.

In terms of an epilogue, the story of Hegewisch came full circle in 2016 when CRRC Sinfang America contracted to build a plant on the old PSC/USRSC property—in order to manufacture railcars.

Please note that street names in Hegewisch have changed three times. In the interests of saving space and eliminating confusion, the names used are the ones current at this writing.

One

THE COMPANY'S TOWN

USRSC's mission was to produce freight cars at a profit. After opening its first plant at Urbana, Ohio, the company realized that Chicago was becoming an important junction of the national railroad business, and so they set up another plant on the South Branch of the Chicago River. Within a few years, fires and the crowded conditions of the riverbank encouraged the company to relocate. USRSC found 100 acres at the far southeast end of Hyde Park Township on the Calumet River. Although the new location would ensure superior transportation systems, the area hosted only two or three farming families. To provide housing for workers, an additional 1,500 acres north and east of the factory site were purchased by the Hegewisch Land Syndicate, which was a separate legal entity. It laid out streets and subdivisions and then sold the property for residential, commercial, and industrial sites to all comers. Brandon, Baltimore, and Brainard Avenues became the principal commercial streets with the company's gate, located near the intersection of Brandon and Brainard Avenues. Churches, a school, houses, commercial buildings, and boardinghouses soon followed. Like any other industrial firm, USRSC was subject to the vagaries of the national economy. At times business was booming, and jobs were plentiful. When the economy hit a recession, layoffs were numerous, and Hegewisch residents soon learned to depend on other nearby industrial concerns as well as seasonal work to make ends meet. As Hegewisch settled into its routine, USRSC went on to open two more railcar factories, both in Alabama.

It is very difficult to find an example of a 19th-century wooden freight car, let alone one produced by USRSC. Individually, freight cars were cheap to build out of basic materials like wood, cast iron, and steel. Thereafter, never washed, revarnished, or repainted, they had a useful life of approximately 10 years, although they usually survived for 16, quite often ending up as a shed in a remote farm field. About the time USRSC moved to Hegewisch, a good wooden boxcar cost about $500 to build and under ideal conditions would pay for itself in one year, generating a nine percent return for the first five years. Carefully managed and driven hard, the boxcar was one of the greatest moneymakers of the 19th century. Yet a car that swayed and bounced around the country, was loaded and unloaded, and subjected to derailments and bad weather was often sidetracked for repairs or simply lost, therefore not generating income. The above car was owned by the Detroit, Toledo & Ironton Railroad. (Author's collection.)

A boxcar is essentially a bridge on wheels. The bridge or floor frame, which had to support the cargo and withstand the pulling stress of the entire train, was built with eight four-by-eight timbers or sills, which, in turn, were bolted to heavy cross timbers called bolsters. The wheel assembly, called a truck, was made with iron straps, bolts, and castings. In the 1880s, designers began calculating the ratio of stress to the strength of these materials. Although the standard arch-bar truck was rickety and often out of square, it was safe enough at 10 miles per hour, the speed at which existing tracks and bridges could support a 1,000-ton train (approximately 50 cars plus locomotive). Designers also proposed adding more metal to the framing members, while inventors tinkered with air brakes and safer coupling mechanisms. But innovations had to be compatible with the old cars and cost-conscious car builders, such as USRSC at Urbana (above), continued to build boxcars from wood long after steel became the material of choice. (Champaign County Historical Society.)

Although USRSC headquarters were in New York City, the first plant was erected in Urbana, Ohio, above, at a junction of the Erie; the Pittsburgh, Cincinnati, Chicago & St. Louis; and the Cleveland, Cincinnati, Chicago & St. Louis Railroads. Civic leaders and local investors were so excited by the potential financial gain for Urbana that they "donated" the land. John Harris, mill manager in Hegewisch, below, one of the first men hired. He recalled in 1936 that the land purchased from the Calumet and Chicago Canal and Dock Company was so low-lying that when foundations were laid, a slip was dredged off the Calumet River and the spoils dumped behind an embankment. Departments at both locations included a blacksmith shop, paint and erecting shops, and a lumberyard. (Above, Champaign County Historical Society; below, SCHM.)

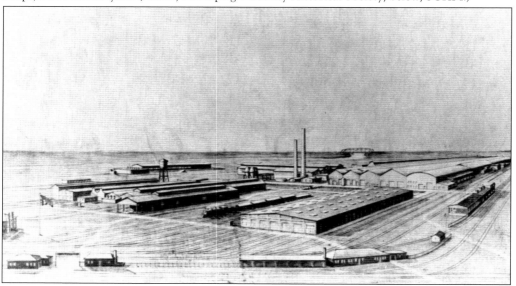

In 1881, the main line of the CWI, which carried the Monon, the Wabash and the Erie Railroads, came to Hegewisch from Pullman Junction between Torrence Avenue and the west shore of the Calumet River. It crossed the river near 126th Street and then ran southeast between the USRSC plant (to the right in this photograph) and Hegewisch to its interlocking tower at the Indiana state line. (SCHM.)

Around the same time as the CWI came through Hegewisch, the South Chicago & Southern ran from South Chicago to Bernice (later Lansing, Illinois). The flagman and his family are shown here at the junction with the CWI. Before mechanical or electrical signals were common, manually operated gates such as these smash boards were positioned to give approaching locomotive engineers the authority to proceed or stop. (SCHM.)

By 1882, the New York Chicago & St. Louis Railroad, commonly known as the Nickel Plate, had made its way through Hegewisch, its right-of-way paralleling the CWI. Here, it is shown in a 1940 photograph, westbound, crossing the Pennsylvania Railroad tracks. The catenary bridges of the Chicago South Shore & South Bend (CSS&SB) can be seen in the background. (Nickel Plate Road Historical & Technical Society.)

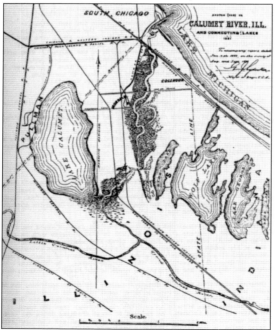

Although USRSC built railcars, it still required water transportation amenities. Like its site in Chicago, the new plant was placed on the water near the junction of the Little, Grand, and Calumet Rivers. The northern limits of the town of Hegewisch included Hyde Lake and Wolf Lake. They combined with the three railroads that girdled the area, physically cutting it off from neighboring settlements. (SCHM.)

Today, Indian Creek runs south of and roughly parallel to 126th Street. In 1889, it drained Wolf Lake through Hyde Lake and into the Calumet River. Pete Hill's tavern and residence was at the northeast corner of Baltimore Avenue near 132nd Street. He also owned a small farm on Carondolet Avenue near the creek, which was then called Pete Hill's Creek. (Author's collection.)

Wolf Lake is essentially a swale, or a depression between dunes that is common to the topography of the Calumet region. Hegewisch is located southwest of the lake. Hyde Lake north of town added to the area's marshiness until it was drained in 1927. In 1883, both lakes contributed to the area's renown as a "hunters' paradise" because of the wildlife they attracted. (Author's collection.)

In a 1936 interview, James Hopkinson recalled that when he moved to Hegewisch in 1884 there were three homesteads: one was a cabin on Burley Avenue across from the Webster School land, one on Baltimore Avenue in the 132nd Street block, and one family farm (above) on Wolf Lake at 128th Street—which the Neubeiser family leased from Charles B. Shedd, secretary and treasurer of the Knickerbocker Ice Company. Fredericka Konybisy (at left) emigrated from Germany to Ohio in the 1850s where she met her future husband, Joe. They married in 1855 and by 1859 were living in a cabin near 134th Street and Burley Avenue. Later, they lived on the Calumet River near 126th Street. Their daughter Annie married August Neubeiser. After she was widowed, Annie and her nine children stayed on the farm, which often served as a hunting resort. (Both, SCHM.)

Among the most "famous" of the farmers in early Hegewisch was Ann Reese. In 1889, she lived at 130th Street and Avenue O, where she maintained an orchard. There were a lot of small farms where the Ford plant stands today on Torrence Avenue and 130th Street. Farming continued into the 20th century, with Ellis Bennett, known mainly for the Delaware House, selling water lilies he raised in the shallows of Wolf Lake. East of that, along 134th Street, there was a small cattle farm. The Struzik family had a truck farm between Avenue O and the lake. The Zylek farm was at 135th Street and Avenue L, and many Arizona (an area east of downtown) families kept cows that were turned out in the prairie east of the neighborhood. The Sicady family used a horse and wagon to deliver hay to the neighborhood cows. Many families also raised a pig every summer. By the late 1930s, most of the milk cows were gone, and families were having milk delivered every morning by Casey Krolak, who would place bottles on fences at the alley. (SCHM.)

HEGEWISCH SUBDIVISIONS.

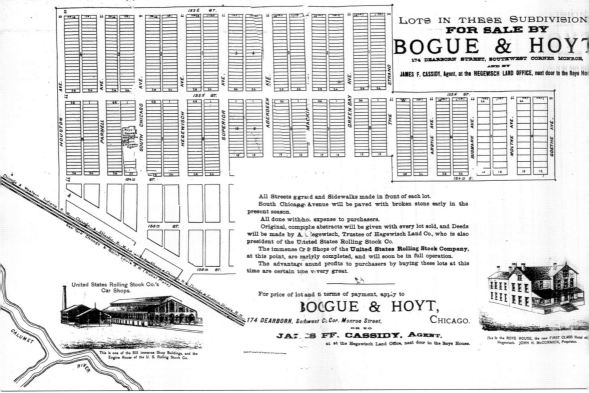

All Streets ggraid and Sidewalks made in front of each lot.

South Chicago Avenue will be paved with broken stone early in the present season.

All done without expense to purchasers.

Original, complete abstracts will be given with every lot sold, and Deeds will be made by A. Hegewisch, Trustee of Hegewisch Land Co., who is also president of the United States Rolling Stock Co.

The immense Car Shops of the **United States Rolling Stock Company**, at this point, are rapidly completed, and will soon be in full operation.

The advantage and profits to purchasers by buying these lots at this time are certain to be very great.

For price of lot and terms of payment, apply to

BOGUE & HOYT,

174 DEARBORN, Southwest Cor. Monroe Street, CHICAGO.

OR TO

JAMES FF. CASSIDY, Agent.

at the Hegewisch Land Office, next door to the Boys House.

The Hegewisch Land Company was responsible for the town of Hegewisch, not the car factory. It was a real estate concern that might direct a client to an architect or a building contractor, but it was not interested in owning houses or commercial buildings. The syndicate of investors included nine men, with three of them being the principals. They were J. William Eschenburg, William H. Rand, and Cyrus D. Roys, who owned 20.5, 25.0, and 12.5 percent of the company respectively. Eschenburg was known in the area because of his "Eschenburg Addition" in North Hammond. C.D. Roys had made his name several years before as the legal counsel for the Lake Shore & Michigan Southern Railroad. Now, he was the vice president of USRSC. These three men made all the decisions for the syndicate members. Adolf Hegewisch was the company's administrator and had no vote. The company's office was located midway between 133rd and 134th Streets on the west side of Baltimore Avenue. (SCHM.)

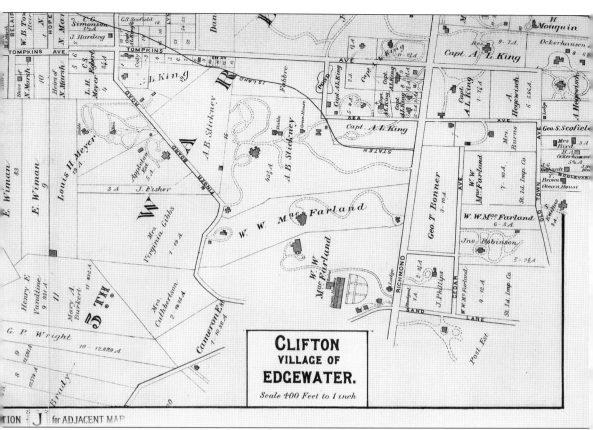

Adolf Hegewisch was born in Mexico in 1843 to German and Spanish parents. Shortly after assuming the presidency of USRSC, he became a naturalized US citizen and later that year brought his wife, Josefa de la Serna, to the United States from Mexico. Their household on Staten Island (upper right, two parcels with circle) included six servants and the families of his two brothers. Hegewisch was a director of the Yonkers Rapid Transit Company, president of a Mexican silver mine, and a stockholder of the Staten Island Rapid Transit Railroad. He also owned property in Chicago near the northeast corner of Torrence Avenue and 130th Street. At this writing, there are no known photographs of Hegewisch. After being relieved of his post as receiver for USRSC during the financial crisis of 1890, he disappeared from the public record in New York. Around 1900, he was found to be the manager of the American Bank of the City of Mexico, where he died in 1912. (Author's collection.)

St. Columba Church,
133 and Green Bay Avenue,
Hegewisch, Ill.

Fr. Timothy O'Sullivan said the first Mass at St. Columba church in November 1884. He had also organized St. Kevin's in South Deering (105th Street and Torrence Avenue) in the spring of that year. Located at 133rd Street and Greenbay Avenue, St. Columba served the mostly Irish and Swedish residents of the newly settled Hegewisch. Reverend Chodniewicz, above, was pastor around 1904. (SCHM.)

In 1885, the Hegewisch Methodist Episcopal Church began meeting in a room over a store on Brainard Avenue under the leadership of Rev. Luke Hitchcock. Shortly thereafter, the congregation built a small church at 13315 South Brandon Avenue. In 1905, the congregation sold that building and held services in the Opera House, while the Ladies Aid Society and the Epworth League raised funds to complete the new church at 13501 Burley Avenue in 1906. (SCHM.)

In 1885, John Harris called a citizens' meeting to which he invited Adolf Hegewisch to discuss the need for a school. Through Hegewisch, the land company donated the entire block between 133rd and 132nd Streets and Buffalo and Burley Avenues to the Hyde Park school district. The Daniel Webster School was built for $35,000 in 1886 with a Miss Close as the first principal plus six teachers. (SCHM.)

The first fire company in Hegewisch was entirely a volunteer unit with a station on the southeast corner of 135th Street and Burley Avenue. A wheeled hand pump was loaned to Hegewisch by the Hyde Park village board. After annexation, the city built the still-standing Prairie-style structure on the northeast corner. The neighborhood's police station was located at 134th Street and Brandon Avenue and later moved to Baltimore Avenue, south of 134th Street. (SCHM.)

A couple of doors north of the Roys House Hotel was Arcade Hall, constructed in 1888. Adolf Hegewisch was asked to locate the South Chicago & Southern train station and also to build a hall on 133rd Street. In the 1920s, the Arcade became the home of Hegewisch's Fred Schweitzer American Legion Post 272. (Author's collection.)

The Opera House opened in 1888 at 133rd Street and Baltimore Avenue. Over the years, it presented dramas and musicals and hosted church services for new congregations. The Opera House Buffet, the post office, and Hudson and Marcy's meat market were on the ground floor. The entry at the corner was built on an angle, as were the entrances of the other three corner structures at the intersection. (SCHM.)

From the earliest days, women were part of Hegewisch's commercial and cultural activities. Out of 43 boardinghouses located close to the USRSC gate, 23 were run by women. In the same neighborhood, Annie Meselli provided laundry service for the men who rented rooms. Mary Elijah, a dressmaker located on 133rd Street between Brandon and Burley Avenues, billed her business as a "fashionable cloak and dress maker." The Franciscan Sisters of Chicago came to town in 1908 to teach at St. Florian's. Helen (Fleming) Czachorski was an attorney from Buffalo, New York, who practiced in Hegewisch for over 50 years. In 1958, she was sworn in before the US Supreme Court, which allowed her to practice law before it. The first principal at the Webster School/Henry Clay Elementary School was a Miss Close. Over the years, most of the school's teachers were women, including Esther Sipple, who taught at Henry Clay Elementary School for 34 years. Her sister Edna was a Hegewisch insurance agent. Other women partnered with their husbands to operate neighborhood businesses such as Ethel and Jacob Brody, above, of the Hegewisch Fair Store. (SCHM.)

Work in early Hegewisch was subject to all the national economic downturns, so some men became market hunters, trapping muskrats and hunting waterfowl around Wolf Lake. Fish were plentiful and could provide meals for the family. Although the federal government had already begun setting limits on hunting for profit, well into the 1930s, at 4:30 a.m. most days, WLS radio's "Johnny Muskrat" announced the current price for muskrat skins. (SCHM.)

Ice cutting was a seasonal job. The Shedd cousins' Knickerbocker Ice Company was on Wolf Lake around 130th Street. Men with tongs and horses pulled the ice blocks out of the water and dragged them to the icehouse, a long, narrow barn filled with hay or sawdust. Ice was sold to cool refrigerated freight cars as well as to home and tavern iceboxes. (Hammond Public Library Local History Room.)

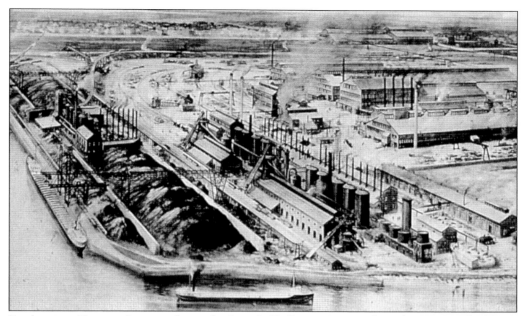

By the time Hegewisch came along, the Joseph H. Brown Iron and Steel Company had been operating at 106th Street and the Calumet River since 1875. Joseph Thatcher Torrence, one of the founders, was also the general manager and the street that later connected Hegewisch with South Deering was named for him. Once public transportation was set up, the mill provided work for many Hegewisch men. (SCHM.)

The George H. Hammond meatpacking plant opened in 1869 on the south side of the Grand Calumet River in Hammond, Indiana. It was not a short walk from Hegewisch, but many men chose to work there and followed the Nickel Plate tracks and bridge over the river. (Hammond Public Library Local History Room.)

Once the Hegewisch plant was up and running and the town itself was in development, Adolf Hegewisch was sent to Alabama to open a similar operation in Anniston. At the time, Anniston was billing itself as the "Model City," that is, a prime example of Southern post–Civil War recovery. Anniston also provided access to the pine forests of northeastern Alabama where USRSC purchased a significant stand of trees because boxcars were still being built with wood. In 1886, Decatur, in the northwest corner of Alabama on the Tennessee River, was also feeling its oats. At a junction of north-south and east-west southern rail lines, Decatur and thus USRSC were on the Louisville & Nashville line and in a good position to provide rolling stock for that and other Southern railroads such as the Central Railroad of Georgia. (Public Library of Anniston-Calhoun County, Alabama Room Collection.)

Two

ANNEXATION THROUGH WORLD WAR I

The entire township of Hyde Park was annexed to Chicago in 1889, including Hegewisch. So now, although most of the men worked at USRSC, the outlook of the town itself became concentrated on the city of Chicago. USRSC was no longer responsible for infrastructure and other public amenities, which were now up to the city to provide. The town grew slowly with its business area along the Brainard/Baltimore/Brandon axis. Residential areas fanned out from these streets to the west, north, and east.

It was during this period that the north-south street names changed twice. South Chicago became Erie then Baltimore Avenue; Hegewisch became Ontario then Brandon Avenue; Superior became Burley Avenue; Aberdeen became Buffalo Avenue; Mackinaw and Greenbay Avenues remained the same; and Howard became Brainard Avenue. In Arizona, the Strand became Avenue O; Argyle became Avenue N; Bismark became Avenue M; Moltke became Avenue L; and Goethe became Avenue K.

West of downtown, Houston Avenue became Carondolet Avenue and Parnell Avenue became Houston Avenue.

Sociologists like to say that Hegewisch was demographically established by 1920 and there was little change in ethnicities and population numbers between then and 1994. Early residents of Hegewisch were mainly of British and Scandinavian extraction. Within a decade of annexation, Poles, other Slavs, Greeks, Italians, and Jews were hobnobbing with each other. Housing was predominantly one-story, single-family frame buildings with a smattering of apartments until the decade after World War II when brick bungalows began to appear in subdivisions and as fill-ins in existing neighborhoods.

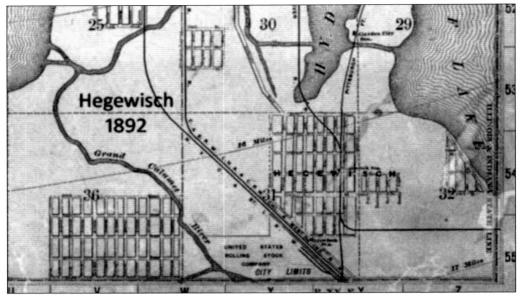

It took two votes, but by the end of 1889, Hyde Park Township and Hegewisch had become part of the city of Chicago. The new city limits were about a mile south of the town, separating it from Burnham, Illinois. The ell of streets to the right on this 1892 map is Arizona. Hegewisch had two train stations, with railroads and waterways surrounding both the town and the USRSC plant. (SCHM.)

In the 1880s and 1890s, Hegewisch had its own newspaper called the *Hegewisch Journal*. It was operated by Thomas and William Barratt with offices on Baltimore Avenue. In the 1880s, the news pertained to Hegewisch doings, whereas in the 1890s, after annexation, the office moved into downtown Chicago, and the news was less about local events and more of a "wire service" nature. (Author's collection.)

In 1893, Chicago hosted the World's Columbian Exposition on Lake Michigan at Hyde Park. After it closed, most of the buildings were put up for sale. A Hyde Park carpenter by the name of Ellis Bennett bought the Delaware State House and had it transported by barge to the site he had chosen on Wolf Lake, approximately where Avenue N ends today. Continuing the area's "hunters' paradise" tradition, Bennett and his wife, Julia, hosted hunting and fishing parties and raised water lilies for sale. However, Bennett did not own the property. It was part of the Charles B. Shedd estate, and so when Shedd evicted him, there was some gunfire and then a court battle. Bennett lost and moved to Washington state to live with his daughter. Hegewisch tavern keepers Josephine and Barney Glinski bought the Delaware State House. For a time, Josephine Glinski lived there, and locals remembered going to picnics at Delaware Grove in the 1930s. Josephine Glinski died in 1956, and soon after, the building was demolished. (SCHM.)

J. William Eschenburg continued to advertise that he promoted land on both sides of the state line, "in the center between Hegewisch and East Chicago." His State Line Additions contained 1,100 lots, which variously abutted the right-of-ways of the CWI, Chicago & Atlantic, the Nickel Plate, the Monon, and the Chicago & Calumet Terminal railways and fronted Gostlin Avenue, which was 80 feet wide and macadamized so residents or business owners could travel with ease from East Chicago through Hammond and Hegewisch all the way to South Deering and South Chicago. Known on maps as Brunswick, German locals often called the north Hammond subdivision "Bethlehem." On the corner of Gostlin and Dearborn Avenues was Rippe's Tavern (above). On the vacant lots to the west of the establishment, Henry Rippe, First Ward alderman of Hammond, hosted picnics with beer and bands and the occasional circus. His Sunday picnics attracted folks from north Hammond and Hegewisch as well as disapproving Hammond clergy. (Author's collection.)

In the 1889–1890 local directory, Daniel Jordan was mentioned as being a carpenter at USRSC. By 1896, he and Henry Lammering were dealing in coal, wood, and ice plus teaming and moving at 13352 Brandon Avenue. After annexation, Jordan joined a committee to petition the city for water pressure, which resulted in the installation of a pumping station. In the 1920s, Jordan was president of the Hegewisch State Bank and also owned Jordan's Hall at 13304 Baltimore Avenue. (SCHM.)

Baltimore Avenue was anchored by the Opera House, the turreted building on the left, at 133rd Street. Restaurants, groceries, dry goods stores, and taverns lined the street. Early Hegewisch was a walking town, and shops like these were conveniently located within a block or two of where customers lived. They often had apartments above them, too. The little police station was one block south, and boardinghouses filled in the next block close to the plant entrance. (SCHM.)

Klucker's Pharmacy opened in Hegewisch in 1888 at 13332 Baltimore Avenue. The building was destroyed by fire in 1947, and the business moved to the corner at 13300 Baltimore Avenue where it became a neighborhood landmark. Originally operated by Albert C. Klucker, Albert Jr. took over in 1941, eventually passing it to his son Harold. Over the years, Klucker's not only filled prescriptions, but sold paperback books, magazines, perfumes, and other gift items as well. (SCHM.)

Fleischmann's saloon, pictured here around 1900 at the corner of 133rd Street and Brandon Avenue, was common in Hegewisch with the bar and package goods sales in front, living quarters upstairs, and another retail space at the back. The side door toward the back was the family entrance to the tavern with tables and chairs. Fleischmann's was a tied house, required to sell Seip products. (Michael Aniol.)

Saloons were always a part of the commercial fabric of Hegewisch, with many of the original operators using their savings to open other businesses. The building that housed Binkowski's tavern at 13260 Baltimore Avenue, shown at right, later became First Savings & Loan of Hegewisch, locally known as Ginalski's. Vincent Ginalski, the savings and loan founder, was the grandson of John Binkowski. (SCHM.)

Around 1900, 133rd Street (looking west) was still "paved" with sand. In 1883, there had been talk of digging the canal here, which would have connected the Calumet River with Wolf Lake. On the right is the building that later became Baginski's Pharmacy on Brandon Avenue. A block beyond, on the corner of Baltimore Avenue, is Binkowski's. (SCHM.)

Germans were among the earliest residents of Hegewisch. By 1892, they had organized Trinity Lutheran Church, which was a member of the Missouri Synod. Their first building was on Houston Avenue. In 1922, the congregation moved to 13200 Burley Avenue. Many non-Lutherans attended the Christmas Eve service at Trinity because it had an exceptional choir. (SCHM.)

The Swedish Lutheran of Hegewisch began meeting in 1895 at Nelson's Feed Store to form a congregation. By Christmas 1896, they had built themselves a church at 13159 Brandon Avenue. Officially, it was the Swedish Evangelical Lebanon Lutheran Church, but over time it became known simply as the "Swedish Church." A Mr. Blomquist was the first preacher, and Sunday school included lessons in the Swedish language. (SCHM.)

Once Hegewisch had been annexed to Chicago, the city's school board took over the Webster School and renamed it for Henry Clay. The school was located in the next block east of Fleischman's on Burley Avenue. The children here are from two classes and are pictured with the teacher, a Miss Krietwitz (right), in 1906. (SCHM.)

The Henry Clay Elementary School faculty in the spring of 1906 included the principal, a Mr. Monahan (first row, right), and Samuel Martindale (second row, left), custodian and truant officer. The teachers are, from left to right, (first row) unidentified, a Miss Krietwitz, and a Miss Lamb; (second row) a Miss Maxey, unidentified, unidentified, and Mary Jabrosky. (SCHM.)

Although Masses were regularly said in Polish at St. Columba church, in 1905, ninety-seven families organized St. Florian parish to build a church at the northeast corner of 132nd Street and Houston Avenue (above, right). A short time later, the parish had its own parochial school in a building with eight classrooms (brick structure behind the church). The Sisters of St. Francis of Chicago took on teaching duties in 1908. (SCHM.)

By the 1916–1917 school year, the Webster School had been deemed a fire trap. The Chicago Board of Education tore it down and built Henry Clay Elementary School in its place. The school had the first Parent-Teacher Association (PTA) in Chicago. When recess was over, the boys filed in through one side door and the girls through the other while a student played marches on the piano. (SCHM.)

In 1908, Hegewisch's first Chicago South Shore & South Bend (CSS&SB) train station on Brainard Avenue at Brandon Avenue was at the back of a building, which also housed a tavern and rooming house. The only station on the new Kensington & Eastern line built to connect Indiana with the Kensington station, it had oak floors, an oak cubicle for the ticket office, an oak snack counter, and a large potbellied stove. (SCHM.)

The first CSS&SB railroad bridge to span the Little Calumet River at 130th Street was a swing bridge with the tender's hut on top of the center pier. In August 1908, while it was still under construction by the American Bridge Company, the structure was blown up with dynamite. Reports at the time hinted that this was the "work of someone unfriendly toward non-union" workers. (SCHM.)

"The Durable Dane," Oscar Matthew "Battling" Nelson was Hegewisch's "Favorite Son" for most of the 20th century. Born in 1882 in Denmark, he and his family arrived in Hegewisch around 1886. At a circus performance in 1896, he decided to give boxing a try. He beat the "Terrible Unknown" and won $5. Although his father forbade him to fight, the boxing bug had bit. Nelson left home and gained experience and weight. Turning professional in 1900, he became known for his phenomenal stamina. In Goldfield, Nevada, in 1906, Nelson beat Joe Gans in 42 rounds to become the Lightweight Champion of the World. The brutality of boxing caught up with him in 1910 when he fought Ad Wolgast to defend his title and lost in the 40th round of a "murderous mauling." Nelson was never the same again. After a 21-year career, he retired in 1917 and published his autobiography *Life, Battles and Career of Battling Nelson, Lightweight Champion of the World*. He died at age 71 in 1954. In 1957, Nelson was inducted into the Boxing Hall of Fame. (SCHM.)

Sipple Brothers, located three doors north of 132nd Street on Baltimore Avenue in the 1890s, sold groceries, crockery, and glassware. William (right) organized and cashiered for the Hegewisch State Bank for 25 years. His son Irwin was an attorney in Hegewisch for 44 years. His daughter Esther taught at Henry Clay Elementary School for 34 years, and another daughter Edna sold insurance and real estate at 13350 Brandon Avenue. (SCHM.)

Among Hegewisch's early financial institutions was the Interstate National Bank at 13310 Baltimore Avenue. The building was designed by Parker Noble Berry as his first commission after leaving the office of Louis Sullivan in Chicago in 1917. Founded in 1907, Interstate National stopped printing bank notes in 1927. The two-story commercial building that later replaced it, incorporated its decorative terra-cotta frieze into the facade. (University of Minnesota.)

Founded in 1899, General Chemical built its plant north of Hegewisch, near the Calumet River, at 12261 Carondolet Avenue in 1903. Locals called it "Chemical," and its address was "Chemical Road." There were houses at 123rd Street and Carondolet Avenue for managers so that they would be close by in case of emergencies. In 1920, General Chemical became a division of Allied Chemical and Dye Corporation. (Author's collection.)

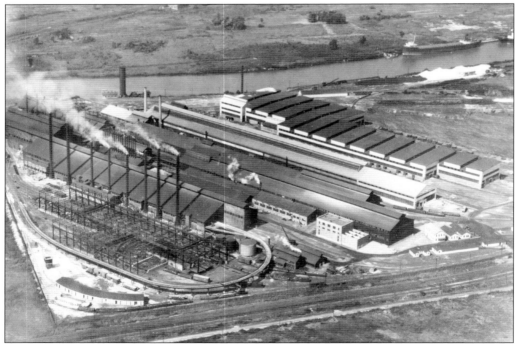

The Grand Crossing Tack Company was organized in 1883 to produce carpet tacks. By 1902, it was prosperous enough to create its own steel mill on the east side of the Calumet River at 118th Street. In 1916, it was bought by Interstate Iron and Steel of East Chicago, becoming part of the Republic Steel Corporation in 1930. The mill provided another option for Hegewisch workers who commuted by streetcar. (SCHM.)

This is the yard at Western Steel Car and Foundry Co. (WSCF), which leased and occupied the USRSC site in 1902. In and out of bankruptcy in the 1890s, USRSC had done business as US Car, then Illinois Car, and finally Western Steel. In the background of the photograph above is the tree line of the Grand Calumet River. The age of the wooden freight car was over, and the photograph below shows the steel hopper car assembly line using plates, wheels, trucks, merchant bars, billets, bolts, splice bars, etc. produced by Chicago-area steel mills. By 1906–1907, WSCF was using 40,000 tons of steel a month. In 1912, WSCF exercised its option to purchase USRSC. It, in turn, was absorbed by Pressed Steel Car Co. in 1926 and thereafter known in Hegewisch as Pressed Steel. (Both, SCHM.)

Most manufacturing companies of the day made some effort to provide "perks" for their employees. There were employee bands, baseballs teams, and some even offered reading rooms or branches of the Chicago Public Library. Here, around 1918, Western Steel Car and Foundry employees enjoy a picnic on a day off. (SCHM.)

By 1900, the rolling stock industry was solidly planted in the Calumet Region with factories all along the southern shore of Lake Michigan. In 1906, William Ryan, manager of Western Steel Car and Foundry, bought the nearby Northwestern Car and Locomotive. Renamed Ryan Car (above), the business was primarily a car rebuilder, while its subsidiary Camel Company, also in Hegewisch, made car parts and equipment, including pressed steel car ends. (SCHM.)

The image above illustrates the nature of Hegewisch's isolation. To get to Republic Steel (upper left in image below), the East Side, or to South Chicago, the Brandon-Ewing streetcar had to cross Hyde Lake. Laying rails across the lake and then south on Brandon Avenue to the South Shore station on Brainard Avenue was completed just before World War I began. A ride in an unheated car during a snowstorm was uncomfortable, but it was better than walking. On the other hand, motion sickness was not uncommon, and some passengers got off on 118th Street and walked the rest of the way to Hegewisch down Avenue O. On the East Side and in South Chicago, Hegewisch riders could make connections for points farther north in Chicago as well as to Whiting and East Chicago, Indiana. (Both, Michael Aniol.)

A streetcar is approaching the corner of Brandon Avenue and 133rd Street. Running on tracks imbedded in brick pavers, the car's arrival was marked by the clang of a bell. The children waiting in front of the Zacharias Building may have placed metal bottle caps or pennies on the track for the car to smash. The building was later home to Bernardi's Ice Cream Parlor. (Michael Aniol.)

Once the Hegewisch Land Company closed, other real estate agents moved in to sell lots on streets such as Brandon Avenue, above. Between 1889 and 1917, there were at least 12 such firms, mostly on Baltimore Avenue. Swedish immigrant Ben Anderson worked as a machinist until he had enough money to open a real estate office, which years later became Hegewisch Federal Savings & Loan Association of Chicago. (SCHM.)

In the days before paved streets, Baltimore Avenue's main shopping district ran north to south between 132nd Street and Brainard Avenue near USRSC. Stores offered baked goods, brushes, blacksmithing, furniture, barbering, boots, and shoes. There were two dry goods emporiums as well as a dentist, Dr. T. Edwin Bell, in the Opera House. E. Hurd, a dressmaker, had her shop down the street. (SCHM.)

Dr. Jacob Poehls was the local physician and surgeon in the early days of Hegewisch. His house (above) was located on Baltimore Avenue near Brainard Avenue not far from the USRSC plant. As an integral part of the medical community, the following midwives served Hegewisch into the World War I era: Maria Bloomberg, Susan Berenz, Ida Bock, Marie Skatula, Anna Dziengel, Katherina Keiffer, Julie Kieniz, and Mary Wojtas. (SCHM.)

Although the industrial might of the United States during World War II is well known, the role of American manufacturers like Western Steel in the Great War is often overlooked. America produced millions of artillery projectiles (above), first for the European Allies and later for US troops, when the Americans were supplied with French artillery. Munitions production became a competition that the Germans called *Materialschlachte* or "battle of materials." (Michael Aniol.)

Like many industrial firms, Western Steel provided a certain number of extracurricular activities for its employees. The Hegewisch plant had a band, and here, the workforce has gathered as part of a World War I Liberty bond rally. Through the selling of bonds, the US government raised around $17 billion for the war effort and introduced many workers to the idea of buying financial securities. (Michael Aniol.)

There was a strong home front effort in Hegewisch during World War I, as evidenced by this parade down Baltimore Avenue. Along with meatless and wheatless days, people bought Liberty bonds to support the Allied cause, and these purchases became a symbol of patriotism. Boy Scouts, Girl Scouts, and Camp Fire Girls joined in the rallies to support the troops. (SCHM.)

The downside to wartime parades and rallies was death. Killed near Verdun, France, on October 14, 1918, Sgt. Fred Schweitzer of Company D, 125th Infantry, American Expeditionary Forces was the only Hegewisch casualty of the war. Schweitzer's body was returned to the United States in 1921. American Legion Post 272, housed in the Arcade Building at 13304 Baltimore Avenue, was dedicated to him in 1922. (Author's collection.)

Most of the houses in Arizona (above) were built by Western Steel on corner post foundations. Later, they were lifted on jacks while concrete was poured and block walls were laid, then lowered onto their basements. Because these houses went up before the streets were paved and sewers put in, water was available only from a well. Neighborhood stores soon came along selling everything from bread and butter to dishes and coffee to meat and vegetables. And the storekeeper probably spoke the language of the neighborhood. For banking, dry goods, a movie, church, and school, residents had to walk into Hegewisch. On 133rd Street, they would have passed this row of houses (below) a block away from Henry Clay Elementary School. The typical Hegewisch neighborhood was one of modest houses interspersed with apartment buildings. (Both, author's collection.)

Three

POSTWAR BOOM

Hegewisch had and has a great tavern tradition. Unlike that other company town, Pullman, there was no such thing as "dry" in Hegewisch. Saloons were put up as quickly as boardinghouses near the intersection of Brandon Avenue with 135th Street, Brainard Avenue, and the USRSC gate. When Prohibition was inaugurated, the saloons became "soft drink" bars. Being so close to the Indiana state line, a certain amount of bootlegging went on, and 134th Street was often called "Bootleg Alley."

After World War I, civic improvements resumed. In 1922, the Cal-Sag Channel was completed, and Hegewisch, along with the rest of the southeast side and the south suburbs, became part of a drainage district, which alleviated flooding and insured clean drinking water coming from Lake Michigan. By the 1920s, the ethnic makeup of the town had stabilized with Poles leading the numbers. Small businesses thrived, including the opening of automobile dealerships and new industries. As was the case throughout the nation in the 1920s, Hegewisch experienced a building boom, particularly on the west side or "behind the park" streets of Muskegon, Manistee, and Saginaw with brick bungalows and two- and three-flat apartment buildings. In a few instances, the new structures combined business with residential space where "mom and pop" lived "over the store" either in the middle of the block or at a corner. Despite the advent of the automobile, Hegewisch was still a walking town. The population in 1920 was pegged at 4,207. By 1930, it was 7,890.

Joseph Pavich, a Dalmatian immigrant, bought the tavern and buildings at 13257–13259 South Baltimore Avenue in 1921. Part of the Hegewisch Land Company, the property had changed hands many times between 1884 and 1911, when it was purchased from Frank and Lillie Kohn by Robert Uihlein of the Joseph Schlitz Brewing Co. Thereafter it was a tied house, meaning the leasing tavern keeper was required to sell only Schlitz products. The Schiltz bannered-globe logo was raised on the building's parapet. Later renters were Jan Piatek, Andrew B. Konieczny, Kurnik & Sanecki, and Walter Bubacz. In 1919, while Joe Pavich was part-owner (with a cousin) of a saloon near the intersection of Wentworth Avenue and Twenty-second Street in Chicago, Prohibition took effect. Undoubtedly cutting a good deal with the Uihlein family, Pavich, his wife, five children, and mother-in-law moved to the apartment upstairs. Along with selling "soft drinks," he was able to rent out the small building behind the tavern and one to the north, which got him through Prohibition—that and probably some winemaking in the cellar beneath the saloon. (Author's collection.)

Moll's restaurant in the stylish building at 13358 Houston Avenue was later remembered as a place "you got dressed up for Friday night dinner." Other Moll businesses were Moll's Gas & Oil Service Station, also known as Triangle Service Station, at 134th Street and Carondolet Avenue, and the George Moll tavern at 13258 Houston Avenue. The restaurant was shuttered in the mid-1960s when "the owner just closed the door one day." (SCHM.)

The Triangle Hotel at 13542 Brandon Avenue was located at the end of the line for the 108th/Ewing streetcar at 136th Street and Brainard Avenue. Built in 1923, it was owned by Ely and Annie Zorich. Nick Grapsas, who operated the concession in the South Shore station across the street, and other Greek immigrants often lived at the hotel until their families arrived from Europe. (Author's collection.)

Although the North Shore Channel of the Sanitary District of Chicago was in operation in 1912, the Cal-Sag Channel, which would drain Hegewisch, was not opened until 1922. Carrying pollution away from Lake Michigan, it also made the rivers around Hegewisch navigable for larger vessels and connected the Great Lakes to the Gulf of Mexico in a practical way. In 1920, A.R. Harris, president of the Hegewisch Chamber of Commerce, was instrumental in securing sewers, streets, water service, phone service, and the opening of 134th Street, above, between Avenue K and Sheffield Avenue (in Hammond). Known as the "Dump Road" because the marsh on its north side was slowly filled with slag from the mills and refuse from the city, in the 1920s, it was also known as "Bootlegger Alley" and "Booze Alley" due to its isolation and lack of streetlights (which ended at the state line). Fisher's Camp, located down the Indiana Harbor Belt tracks (at left), rented boats during the summer and was also reportedly a source of bootleg beer. (Author's collection.)

As more Greeks arrived in Hegewisch and either brought or started families, the need for a local church was felt. The Assumption Greek Orthodox Church was founded in 1924. Reverend Dimitriadis was the pastor. The church opened for services in 1926 around Burley and Buffalo Avenues and 136th Street. This building burned in 1936. The one located today on Brainard Avenue near 136th Street was dedicated in 1937. (Author's collection.)

This formal photograph was taken of Lucie Pavich with her confirmation godmother Dina Manghera after the ceremony at St. Columba church. Although St. Columba parish had been in Hegewisch since 1884, its first recorded First Communion ceremony took place in 1921 with 73 communicants. Its first confirmations took place in 1928, with records showing that 117 children participated. (Author's collection.)

The above booklet commemorates a Henry Clay Elementary School PTA–sponsored open house around 1927 and tells of the day's program, which featured musical performances and artwork by the students. The assistant superintendent of schools, Rose A. Pesta, gave the main address. She was followed by the introduction of former principals, members of the PTA, and the Hegewisch Businessmen's Association. Henry Clay Elementary School sponsored the first PTA in the city. In the 1920s, Henry Clay Elementary School and St. Florian School were the only options for elementary education. However, many of the churches offered Sunday school classes that included lessons in the language of the community, e.g., German, Swedish, or Greek. Children of the Jewish faith often attended Sabbath school either in South Chicago or at a synagogue in Hammond. The synagogue at Hammond was constructed on Sibley Street in 1902. It is a little known fact that Trinity Lutheran Church had a Christian day school under the aegis of the Reverend Louis Millies between 1901 and 1911. (Author's collection.)

There was always music in Hegewisch, from the 1890s with the four-member Hegewisch Mandolin Club to the mid-1920s when Vivian Vico (right) was teaching piano to local youngsters upstairs from her father's haberdashery at 13307 Baltimore Avenue. Over on Houston Avenue, John C. Smolen taught music, too, and billed himself as a concert violinist. Michael Kwilosz at 13319 Baltimore Avenue sold musical instruments as well as jewelry. (Author's collection.)

Elsewhere in town, musicians got together on weekends to play at parties and weddings. This group from the Arizona neighborhood was probably all Polish. The man with the violin on the far right is Joseph M. Ogorek. His son Walter followed in his footsteps by starting as the quartet's drone on violin. Later, Walter switched to clarinet and saxophone, playing with The Campus Boys dance band in the 1930s. (Author's collection.)

The Interstate National Bank was vacated in the late 1920s. The Panayotovich family bought the building, tore it down, and constructed this apartment house. One tenant recalled there were three apartments on the second floor and that it was a "buzzer building," meaning no one could go up to the apartments without being let in by a tenant who signaled that the door was open by sounding a buzzer. (SCHM.)

Among the businesses on Brandon Avenue was the Polska Apteka pharmacy and residence of Dr. John and Helen (Fleming) Czachorski at 13300–13304 Brandon Avenue. They moved there in 1916. While the doctor saw his patients, Helen practiced law in Chicago and later with both of her sons, John F. and Eugene J. The latter was also the editor and publisher of the *Hegewisch News*. (SCHM.)

Poulos and Murphy's grocery opened on the corner of 136th Street and Burley Avenue in the era when a grocer took merchandise from the shelf behind him at the request of the customer. The neighborhood kids of the 1920s loved to shop at Poulos and Murphy's because the business carried Fudgecicles and other treats. The store later moved to the 132nd block of Baltimore Avenue where it was known as Murphy's. (Author's collection.)

Olejniczak's funeral parlor at 133rd Street and Houston Avenue was built in the 1920s and has had several names, including Sadowski's, Lesniak's, and the Joseph Memorial Chapel. Other undertakers in town were August J. Kortas at 13258 Baltimore Avenue around 1939 and Gustave Korthaus on Brandon Avenue from 1900 to 1943. Olejniczak's at one time hosted a branch of the Chicago Public Library, a common practice in the 1920s. (Michael Aniol.)

"Ford City" became a catchphrase around Hegewisch once the Ford plant went up in 1923 at 126th Street and Torrence Avenue. The assembly line building (above) was designed by Albert Kahn, who also designed the hangar at Lansing (Illinois) airport, formerly Ford Field. Many Hegewisch entrepreneurs adopted the Ford name, such as the Ford City Service Station at 13000 Torrence Avenue, Ford City Grill near the same corner, and Ford City Garage at 13421 Brainard Avenue. There was also a Ford dealership at 13303 Baltimore Avenue. The residential area around 130th Street and Marquette Avenue was nicknamed "Ford City" as Chicago real estate developer Axel Lonnquist envisioned a neighborhood south of 130th Street and west of Mann Park full of brick bungalows and three flats such as these. About half-dozen were built before the boom times ended. (Above, Calumet City Historical Society; below, author's collection.)

The Hegewisch station of the South Chicago & Southern Railroad, later the Pennsylvania Railroad, was located at 133rd Street and Mackinaw Avenue on the west side of the tracks. It served passengers until the late 1920s. Peter Neilsen's restaurant was across the street around 1889, and the St. Columba church was a block away. By crossing the tracks eastward, one was entering Arizona, given the nickname because the area was so sandy and scrubby that it appeared desertlike. The streets of Arizona, originally named Goethe, Moltke, Bismark, and Argyle, became Avenues K, L, M, and N, respectively. Avenue O was previously known as The Strand because of its proximity to Wolf Lake. As the Arizona neighborhood grew, mom-and-pop stores appeared on Avenues N and M. Iwan's, near the corner of Avenue N and 134th Street, had the "neighborhood telephone." Ziemba's, just north of the corner of 134th Street and Avenue M, was next door to Krupa's tavern, long a neighborhood fixture. Zbinden's was on the northwest corner of Avenue O and 133rd Street. White Eagle Bakery and Zralka's Poultry served the neighborhood along 135th Street. (SCHM.)

Born in Budapest to Polish parents, Frank Sowa (front, third from right) arrived in the United States in 1901, graduating from St. Florian School in 1912. Between 1915 and 1925, he taught reading, writing, and English grammar to adults, and from 1918 into the 1950s, he prepared immigrants for the naturalization process. His "day jobs" included core-maker at Pressed Steel and secretary to Pressed Steel's master mechanic during World War I. Between 1931 and 1934, he studied law. Then, having been a member of the Cook Country Real Estate Board since 1924, he opened the Sowa Realty Company and the South Suburban Currency Exchange on Brandon Avenue. In the late 1930s, Sowa was also president of the Calumet Airport Association and a member of the Chicago Airport Commission. In later years, he led the Hegewisch Federation of Lodges, a civic group that worked to obtain all the amenities to which Hegewisch was entitled but occasionally were overlooked by city hall. In 1965, a list of his achievements and value to the Hegewisch community was read into the Congressional Record. (Author's collection.)

Four

IN A DEPRESSION BUT NOT DEPRESSED

Although the country entered a deep financial depression in late 1929, by the mid-1930s either people were used to the "new frugality" or for the most part did not feel the pinch. Businesses stayed open. People picked coal that fell off the trains along the curve at 136th Street and Avenue O. Most already had gardens and kept small animals like chickens and geese. The children of the immigrants did not let it bother them too much. They went to school. They found jobs here and there. There were always dances to go to with two or three halls in town and others only a streetcar ride away. Mann Park's field house opened in 1932, and sports like tennis and basketball became popular. Church suppers were also popular. In the middle of the decade, the neighborhood movie theater was updated, and in 1936, Hegewisch got its own newspaper. As part of the federal government's New Deal, streets were paved, many for the first time, which also meant sewers in Arizona. The Hegewisch Community Committee was organized as another outlet for youthful energy as well as an aid to families that were experiencing difficulties. General American Aerocoach opened next door to Pressed Steel Car, and Hegewisch was affected by the Republic Steel Strike that took place on Memorial Day 1937.

An early casualty of the Great Depression was the Hegewisch State Bank at 13358 Brandon Avenue. Established in 1919, by late 1931 its board of directors was asking the Illinois state auditor to take over. Walter E. Schmidt was president at the time with A.C. Klucker as vice president. Ben Anderson and Daniel Jordan were among the board members. (Author's collection.)

Postwar, Hegewisch residents liked to have a good time, and several of them arranged parties on pleasure boats that went out of the Harbor Lights Boat Club on the Little Calumet River at 137th Street and Torrence Avenue. Races were also held on the river. The port authority banner referred to a decades-old effort to establish a port on Lake Calumet a few miles downriver from the club. (SCHM.)

The James R. Mann Park field house opened in November 1932, approximately 25 years after the residents of Hegewisch began presenting their case for a public park to the South Park Commission. Covering an entire city block at 130th Street and Carondolet Avenue, Park No. 9 was renamed to honor the late congressman James Mann in 1922. The opening festivities included city dignitaries, decorations, a dance, a parade, and a reception. (SCHM.)

Congressman James R. Mann (1897–1922) is best remembered for the Mann Act of 1910 (also known as the Mann White Slave Traffic Act) and the Mann-Elkins Act, which regulated railroads. Before going to Washington, Mann was a resident of Oakland in the northeast corner of Hyde Park Township. He served as the South Park Commission attorney and as a Chicago alderman from 1892 to 1896. (Library of Congress Harris and Ewing Collection.)

With the field house, Mann Park also got tennis courts. Indoor crafts classes and sports were offered, and the park district hosted citywide baseball and tennis tournaments in the 1930s. The 1936 champion Lottie Lesniak (left) won the American Legion trophy in tennis, while Ann Pavich (right) placed second. (Author's collection.)

Tony Piet was well known in Hegewisch for his baseball prowess. He played for the Pittsburgh Pirates, leading the team in home runs for 1932. His lifetime batting average was .277. The bust on the counter of Aniol's Hardware in Hegewisch was a gift from Piet to his brother John and depicts Tony as he looked in 1935 when he played for the Chicago White Sox. (Author's collection.)

Unusual weather made the headlines across the nation in the 1930s, with the Dust Bowl of the Plains states being the worst. However, Chicago had its share of winter misery. Here are Nick and Joe Pavich shoveling some of the 44-plus inches of snow that fell in 1934; a total of 26.1 inches of it in December alone. A normal winter snowfall averaged 26 inches. (Author's collection.)

Looking like a lighthouse, Beacon Tower was constructed on the northwest corner of Baltimore Avenue and 134th Street in 1936 by Burnham resident and ham radio operator John Serafin. The idea was to open a gas station on the ground floor, a restaurant on the second, and install a radio station on the fifth floor. While painting window frames, he fell and died soon after. The tower was never finished. (SCHM.)

HEGEWISCH NEWS WEEKLY

HEGEWISCH'S OWN NEWSPAPER

VOL. 1 NO. 1   HEGEWISCH NEWS -- WEEKLY   FRIDAY, APRIL 24, 1

BEAT SCORED WITH THE 1st ISSUE OF SEASO

W A Sidewalk Unit 2715 Really Works

A W. P. A. unit of about thirty-five workers swooped down upon the intersection of Buffalo avenue, and 133rd Street and began demolishing the sidewalk on the east side of 133rd Street Friday, April 7 at about 3 p. m. The foreman of the group, when approached by News-Weekly reporter, became extremely taciturn and refused for a while, to even divulge the number of the project.

"You newspaper fellows always say we just stand around don't do any work," he complained" and we don't like it.

"I've got a fine bunch of men here, and they're all good workers, don't want anything in the papers bout us loafing. We work hard."

It's a Boy at Peterson's

The latest addition to the Hegewisch clan of Peterson arrived in our midst Wednesday, March 18, at St. Margaret's Hospital, weighing seven and a quarter pounds. It's a boy and the first child of Mr. and Werner O. Peterson of 13500 Buffalo Ave. The young mother is the former Kathleen Swartz of Hegewisch and is doing nicely, thank you. The brand new paterfamilias, former athlete who startred at basket-ball with Bowen and with several Hegewisch teams, suffered from a slight swelling of the chest for a while, but is improving rapidly. The symptoms are not unusual in such cases as Dr Stanley S. Brown, attending physician, could tell you.

LADIES' AUXILIARY OF LE- GION POST HOLDS DANCE

The Ladies' Auxiliary of the Fred Schweitzer Post No. 272 of

EDITORIAL

"Charity," the old adage says, "Begins at home."

Well might we add: "And so does business."

When the citizen of Hegewisch spends his money out of town he can be reasonably sure that little, if any of it, will ever find its way back to Hegewisch. When he spends his money with Hegewisch business men he can be just as sure that little, if any of it, will ever LEAVE HEGEWISCH!

For when the Hegewisch business man must in turn buy his needs he will buy them in Hegewisch. He, more than any one else, realizes that a free circulation of money locally assures local prosperity. And his future, and the future of his family, is tied up in Hegewisch.

REMEMBER! Money spent in Hegewisch circulates in Hegewisch and adds to the general prosperity of Hegewisch people.

Money spent out of town is gone forever!

A good many people will argue they can save money by buying at widely advertised "Bargain Sales" conducted by out of town department stores. In remote instances this may be true, but as a general rule it isn't.

In the first place shoppers forget to add the cost of carfare and time spent in shopping to the cost of the goods they buy.

In the second place, if for some reason purchases are unsatisfactory and they wish to make adjustments they must pay the car-

Spring Is He Honest

Spring has come to Hegew (Scoop!)

Yes indeed, signs of that w season of the year are everyw and we are proud to be the to the street with spot news such amazing proportions any other Hegewisch newspa

Despite the fact the mor seem like winter, at noon i comes summer, and fall re with each sundown, the seaso insist, is spring.

Take a leisurely walk al town Sunday (unless there blizzard) and note what our garden experts and flower fa have accomplished already, rock garden enthusiasts are n ning to stir happily among beloved stones, boulders, fern ered rocks and just plain slag

---

Founded in the spring of 1936 by J.B. "Doc" Simborg and his brother Ed, the *Hegewisch News Weekly* started a tradition in Hegewisch that became a thread joining all the following years as well as people and events in the little neighborhood that felt like a stepchild of Chicago. The weekly, issued on Fridays, served as a clearing house for local events and people, plus Chicago and national items that affected the neighborhood. Doc, who had previously written a Hegewisch column for the *Daily Calumet*, was the paper's business manager. Ed was the publisher with George Cole as editor, Estelle Cole as columnist, and Jerome Yalowitz as associate editor. The biggest story of the first issue was that the federal Public Works Administration and Works Progress Administration were employing 135 men to put in sidewalks and to pave 135th Street from Buffalo Avenue in Hegewisch to Avenue K in Arizona. Avenue O and 134th Street had already been paved, and sidewalks were imprinted with "WPA" and the year. Center stage on the front page was an editorial encouraging all of Hegewisch to "shop local." (Author's collection.)

The management of Republic Steel at 118th Street and the Calumet River was adamant in its resistance to labor unions in the 1930s. It is not known how many Hegewisch people were involved in the march on the plant on Memorial Day 1937, but at day's end, 10 marchers were dead in the prairie due to Chicago police gunfire. The event is still known as the Memorial Day Massacre. One of the fatalities was a Hegewisch man by the name of Otis Jones (13211 Buffalo Avenue). The irony is that Jones worked as a riveter for Fruit Growers Express not Republic Steel. He was shot in the spine while standing on the porch of a nearby home. From San Jose, Illinois, Jones had been living in Hegewisch for a little over two months. Also, from Hegewisch was Leo Wachowicz (13146 Houston Avenue) who served as the demonstration model for Dr. Lawrence Jacques during the inquest to show how bullets entered the bodies of the victims. Dr. Jacques not only witnessed the violence that day, but administered first aid. (SCHM.)

Stanley Sluczewski and his business partner Ed Grady were not daunted by a raging economic depression when they closed the Hegewisch Theatre for renovations in August 1937. The exterior refurbishment included neon, porcelain-faced brick, a rounded canopy, and stainless steel poster cases. The enlarged interior accommodated 450 seats plus restrooms, a new screen and curtain, and air-conditioning. Albert Sowa Plumbing and Walenga Electric were local subcontractors. (SCHM.)

A clever promotion was the weekly program. These fliers let people know the current feature films, plus newsreels, cartoons, and the occasional live acts that came to town. Hegewisch had had moving picture theaters before, namely the Five and Ten Cent Theater at 13407 Brandon Avenue, which was owned by John O. Hohwy. It later became the Ontario Theater, owned by E.C. Grady and S.L. Campbell. (Author's collection.)

JANUARY DANCE

-: Given By The :-:

Allied Organizations

OF HEGEWISCH

Frat Boys—Orioles A. C.—Houston Flyers
Rainbow Aces—Live Wire Club
Young Men's Club

At the - ORIENTAL BALLROOM 13338 Brandon Ave.
Hegewisch, Ill.

Sunday Eve., January 13th, 1935

◆ Music by - *"HAPPY JOE DONOVAN'S"* ◆
And his Blue Ridge Syncopators

Entrée 8 P. M.   Admission 25c

Outside of sports and movies, the most popular entertainment for young people was dancing. Tickets were cheap at venues like Jake's Auditorium and the Oriental Ball Room (previously the Adams Furniture Store at 13338–13340 Brandon Avenue, below). Sponsors were mainly athletic and social clubs with fun names like The Live Wires, Pair of Treys, Young Men's Club, Three Gigolos, Four Nuts, Frat Boys, and Rainbow Aces. Any excuse for a dance was used: Harvest Dance, Halloween Dance, Pre-Advent Dance, Hawaiian Moonlight Dance, Hard Times Dance, Live Wire Frolic Dance, Hotcha Jitney Dance, Sweetheart Dance, Divorce Dance, and the Monstrous Japanese Serpentine Puff 'em Confetti Dance. Local bands that played included Jules & His Broadcasting Clowns, Pryor's Sky Larks, Baker's Foot Warmers, Happy Joe Donovan and His Blue Ridge Syncopators, and Speedy and His Masters of Melodies, to name a few. (Above, SCHM; below, Dean Ubik.)

There is More to This THAN MEETS THE EYE

CARGILL INC.

REPUBLIC STEEL

122 ND ST.

GENERAL CHEMICAL

FORD PLANT

WOLF LAKE

LAWRENCE AV.

MANN PARK

AVENUE O

BRAINARD AVE.

PRESSED STEEL

HYMAN-MICHAELS

AERO COACH

8 TH ST.

Although Mann Park provided all sorts of activities for young and old, the neighborhood felt that children and teenagers needed more one-on-one time. As a result, the Hegewisch Community Committee (HCC, brochure above) was founded in 1938. While providing a place for teens to gather, it also took on social work aspects that could assist the aged, the destitute, and families facing hard times, plus address truancy in the schools. Ann Hamilton was the first executive director. It was noted that because of Hegewisch's isolation from the rest of the city, problems that in another community might be minor became major because of the distances involved to obtain adequate assistance and the lack of communication from Chicago as to where the assistance could be secured. Later, Common Ground, a recreational organization, moved to Hegewisch to help establish a youth center and welfare office at 13415 Brandon Avenue. All in all, the aim of the HCC was to be a community self-help program that developed citizen involvement in order to provide a stronger force of community action on social problems. (SCHM.)

To improve navigation and set the stage for the widening of the Cal-Sag Channel and installation of a lock and dam at Hegewisch, the Calumet River was moved west and straightened (dark curve on left) in 1938. Hegewisch Marsh came later on the land between the river and Torrence Avenue (light vertical line). Pressed Steel at "Old Junction" (lower right) retained only a remnant of its former riverfront. (SCHM.)

With Ford Field being the closest airport to Hegewisch and the municipal airport already overcrowded, 10th Ward alderman William Rowan (left) proposed the building of an airport at the north end of Lake Calumet in 1939. With no power wires or other obstacles in the area, once those 300 acres of water were filled in, there would be plenty of space to accommodate land and amphibian planes. (SCHM.)

Along with business development in downtown Hegewisch, change was occurring in the industrial district. In 1936, General American Transportation Corporation (GATX), through a majority stock purchase, took over Pressed Steel with the intention of producing light-rail passenger coaches. In 1939, GATX purchased the motor coach division of Gar Wood Industries and created General American Aerocoach, next door to Pressed Steel. There, the company developed its Mastercraft series of single-unit, welded-steel tube "Streamline" passenger coaches. GATX dated to 1898 when Max Epstein founded Atlantic Seaboard Dispatch (ASD), a Chicago-based railcar leasing firm. Reorganized in 1902 as the German-American Car Company with a repair and maintenance shop in East Chicago, Indiana, it became General American Tank Car, a publicly traded company, in 1916. At General American Aerocoach, 300 of the new-style motorcoaches were constructed before the plant was converted in 1943 to the production of fuselages and inner wings for the Navy. Bus production resumed postwar until General American Aerocoach ceased operations in Hegewisch in 1952. (Author's collection.)

Five

WAR AND POSTWAR

When the news of the attack on Pearl Harbor and subsequent declaration of war reached Hegewisch, young men went off to war. On the home front, victory gardens abounded and so did ration coupons. The weekly newspaper was commandeered by the Office of Civil Defense, but the writers remained and one of the most popular columns was called On the Home Front, which recounted the goings-on in Hegewisch. Since the paper was available to the men overseas, a lot of the commentary was to let them know how things were going at home. Hegewisch people gave blood by the gallons; Hegewisch men died in battle. In 1941, the average income was $1,777, and a new car would have cost $850. A loaf of bread was 8¢, a gallon of gas—if one could get it—was 12¢, and a gallon of milk cost 54¢.

But eventually it was over. The boys came home. Those who died in service were memorialized, but among the living there were weddings and christenings to attend. There was also a housing shortage facing all these newlyweds. People were moving around the country, and some came to Hegewisch hauling their house trailers behind the family Ford. They found a berth on the east side of town in a place called Island Park Homes on the shores of Wolf Lake.

Army Air Force sergeant Walter Ogorek of 13315 Avenue N had registered with the Selective Service Board 94 in October 1940. After basic training in 1942 and learning how to weld at Chanute Field in Rantoul, Illinois, he was shipped to Hickham Field on Oahu, Hawaii. From there, he went on to serve as a welder at the naval airfield in the Fiji islands. (Author's collection.)

Also from Avenue N, Louise Skalka at age 16 joined the Women's Branch of the US Naval Reserve (WAVES) where she trained as an aviation mechanic. Posted to Pearl Harbor shortly after the port was bombed, she watched Navy divers retrieve bodies of drowned seamen. Her brother Alex was a radio school instructor and later served as master sergeant in two Army armored medical battalions. (Alex Skalka family.)

NEWS WEEKLY

"Hegewisch's Own Newspaper"

PUBLISHED BY THE HEGEWISCH CIVILIAN DEFENSE COUNCIL

3c A COPY
10c A MONTH
DELIVERED BY CARRIER

Volume VIII   HEGEWISCH, ILLINOIS, DECEMBER 31, 1943   Number 8

M THE mmander's sk

the holidays are different ear. We did not expect it to erry Christmas like in other Possibly we weren't even to bother with a Christmas ntil we stopped to think just our Toms, Dicks, or Harrys think of us if we forgot. were thinking of the tree at the friends who came in, e church services they were g this year. They were pray- nat Christmas would be a occasion at home the same were praying that it would ppy for them wherever they Have you ever fully realized hat it means to these boys to that the home folks are car- on as usual? Let us keep up prale on the home front.

Service Men's Center has us for a donation Jan. 5. is the first contribution to de in 1944 and we are hopeful ew Year will outnumber all us records made. Many of ood citizens of Hegewisch not made a donation up to ate. Won't you please start ew Year with your name on st?

cago OCD set excellent rec- n the first three War Loan s. The president and the U. S. ary are asking us to surpass records in the Fourth War Drive.

goal is the sale of at least

Blood Donor Mobile Bank At Mann Park Jan. 18-20

Collection For Service Men's Center Jan. 4

The next collection of cakes for Chicago's Service Men's Centers will be held next Wednesday, Jan. 5, at the OCD office at 3147 E. 133d st., Mrs. Rebecca McKernan, community Service Men's Center chairman, announced this week. The office will be open for contri- butions from 10 a. m. to 8 p. m., Mrs. McKernan said.

In the last months of 1943, Mrs. McKernan pointed out, Hegewisch has been more and more generous in its contributions to the Service Men's Center collections, exceeding

Do Your Part to Help . . . Win The War in '44

Hegewisch Urged To Send Blood To War

By MRS. ANNE SOWA
Community Blood Donor Chairman

A pint of your blood can save life! When you give your bloo through the Red Cross Blood Dono Service, you are giving back lif to some wounded fighting man some man who would if he could grasp your hand and say "Thank you."

On Jan. 18 through the 20th, th

One of the first things to change once the United States entered World War II was the name of the local paper, from *Hegewisch News Weekly* to *News Weekly*, "Hegewisch's Own Newspaper." Published by the Hegewisch Civilian Defense Council, its all-volunteer staff included Vi Tukich (Czachorski), Joe Ciezak, Helen Hwastecki, Irene Stancik, Emily Lindberg, and Harry Jacobsen. The Office of Civilian Defense (OCD) at 3147 East 133rd Street was there to keep up civilian morale, run an information office, offer first aid and firefighting courses, and sponsor bond and blood drives. Its managers coordinated block captains and their volunteers and placed concrete flagpoles around town. The office was also the collection point for donations of cakes, cookies, candy, and cigarettes, which were sent on to servicemen's centers in Chicago. Established in 1943, the OCD had a war emergency radio service, collected kitchen grease and fat for munitions and medical supplies, ran house-to-house sales of war savings bonds, and encouraged the establishment of victory gardens. (Author's collection.)

Holding on to their ration books, the people here were lined up outside the A&P on Baltimore Avenue to buy items that were becoming scarce, such as sugar, coffee, and meat. The OCD coordinated blood drives with Anne Sowa as the community chairwoman in 1943. Agnes Collins ran the If You Can Fight, We Can Write club, which connected civilians with servicemen as pen pals. (SCHM.)

Almost immediately, the Red Cross recruited local women to prepare bandages and dressings for military use. The group that was sponsored by St. Florian Church was organized by Mary Owczarzak (second row, third from left), who also served donuts and coffee at the Draft Station on Torrence Avenue and supervised the packing of gifts for servicemen during the holidays. (Author's collection.)

By the summer of 1940, the US government was discreetly preparing for possible involvement in the war in Europe and how to finance it. A bond program was created, and shortly, defense bonds went on sale. The Series E of these bonds was targeted at individual purchasers. As such, they sold for as little as $18.75 and matured in 10 years, at which time the government would pay the bondholder $25. Larger denominations of between $50 and $1,000 were also available, but for those who found it difficult to buy an entire bond at once, 10¢ savings stamps could be purchased and collected in treasury-approved stamp albums until the recipient had accumulated the price of a bond. The name was changed to war bonds after the Japanese attack on Pearl Harbor on December 7, 1941, which resulted in the United States entering the war. The Hegewisch Office of Civil Defense volunteers went door-to-door selling bonds by successfully capitalizing on the government's promotions like this advertisement, which appeared in the Pressed Steel employe newsletter. (Author's collection.)

The first tank produced (for Great Britain at that time) at Pressed Steel Car (PSC) was finished and ready for inspection by July 1941. The road test for the 28-ton medium armored tank was made the following week with a police escort on Dolton Road between Torrence and Cottage Grove Avenues. This aerial photograph shows the PSC plant as it looked during the war, with a test track in the background. By 1943, PSC had over 3,500 employees, 15 percent of them women. One of them, Minnie Metzger, known as "Transmission Minnie," was the only woman in a crew of five that installed one four-ton tank transmission every day for 10 days running. The M-4 was the standard tank produced by several companies in the United States, including Pullman-Standard Car in Hammond, at a cost of about $75,000. Each vehicle, which carried six guns and seven crew members, could accelerate to 45 miles per hour. By November, PSC had a $48-million order to build Sherman M-4 tanks for the US Army. (SCHM.)

The successful army of the World War II era was the one that had the most, the fastest, and the hardest-hitting tank corps. Metalworking companies like PSC were able to produce the M-4s needed for armored divisions by enlarging their plants and retooling their production lines. Government contracts for artillery pieces like the self-propelled howitzer (above) revived the fortunes of PSC and area subcontractors who provided parts and machine-ready metal. (SCHM.)

In February 1945, WGN Radio in Chicago presented the story of how PSC had earned the Army-Navy "E" Award for outstanding performance in producing materials of war. PSC engineers had arrived in Hegewisch in February 1941 and built a 2,000-foot production line by May. One thousand employees were added, and this crew built 10,000 tanks in less than four years. In fact, PSC earned two "E" Awards. (Dean Ubik.)

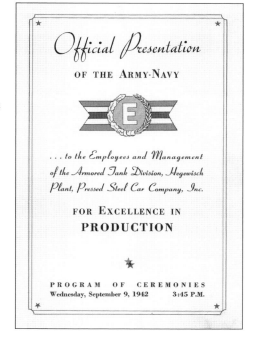

Official Presentation

OF THE ARMY-NAVY

... to the Employees and Management of the Armored Tank Division, Hegewisch Plant, Pressed Steel Car Company, Inc.

FOR EXCELLENCE IN
PRODUCTION

PROGRAM OF CEREMONIES
Wednesday, September 9, 1942   3:45 P.M.

In the summer of 1943, a victory parade was held to boost morale. The reviewing stand was in front of the Office of Civilian Defense at 3147 East 133rd Street, which also housed the Red Cross office. The boys in front of the reviewing stand are members of the Polish Alma Mater Veterans Drum and Bugle Corps, founded by Kinga Skrzekut in 1940. (SCHM.)

Throughout the war, corner memorials were set up to honor the dead from the adjacent neighborhood. Grace Perek remembered that when a new name was to be placed on one, Gene Czachorski would pick her up so that she could play "Taps" on the trumpet for the ceremony. (SCHM.)

World War II took its toll in Hegewisch. The corner memorial and flag shown at right are located at Houston Avenue and 133rd Street to memorialize 2nd Lt. Edward S. Iwan, US Air Corps. The community's first casualty of the war was Gunner's Mate Stanley J. Sukta of the US Navy (below). Lost at sea on November 11, 1942, his name headed the list of war dead in his neighborhood. After the war, the Hegewisch Veterans of Foreign Wars dedicated Post 5414 to him at 13301 Brainard Avenue. In 1946, St. Florian parish raised money to create a memorial plaque and altar for the 25 young men of the parish who died. (Both, SCHM.)

As the war was ending in 1945, the Chicago South Shore & South Bend (CSS&SB) railroad built a new station at Hegewisch. Still located at the junction of Brandon and Brainard Avenues, the building was one story and held a waiting room, restrooms, ticket office, and food concession. Nick Grapsis owned the snack concession. He lived across the street at the Triangle Hotel until his wife and daughter joined him in the early 1950s. (SCHM.)

On a snowy afternoon in 1949, Dorothy Pobereyko waits for her daughter Betty to catch up. Behind her is the sign for Hegewisch Bowling Lanes and Cocktail Lounge, later called Penguin Lanes. The same building at 13338 Brandon Avenue once housed the Adams Furniture Store and the Oriental Ballroom. (Janet Sharko.)

The Hegewisch News

Your Neighborhood Weekly

. 6 — NO. 13   CHICAGO, ILL., JANUARY 12, 1950   FIVE CEN?

m the Editor's atch Pad . . .

TO EXAMINE

e is a growing cry through- nation for a thorough re- sation of our foreign policy esult of the appalling posi- at our country finds itself y.

cry is becoming louder and ng articulation in congress, ess and in mouth to mouth ion. And well it might. us look at the cold, ugly, truth, untainted by propa- or political slant.

Vorld War II we threw our dous weight behind the es opposing Germany be- e war and then entered the nd almost single-handedly at global conflict. We sup- the vast majority of the actured good and food nec. side of our "allies" to do

merged from the war the t single nation on earth. hat did we do? nade a mockery of the lofty that we expounded in the

Hegewisch Man Burns to Death In Stove Blast

A Hegewisch man was burned to death Thursday, Jan. 4, when a kerosene stove used to heat his little residence exploded and show- ered him with flaming kerosene.

The victim is Stanley Kolma, 53, of 13244 Avenue O, who was employed by the Waylite Co., Fire- men called to the scene found Kolma's body near the stove and theorized that the deceased was trying to light the stove when the explosion occurred.

Funeral services for the deceas- ed were held Saturday, Jan. 6, at St. Florian church. Interment fol- lowed at Holy Cross cemetery. The Opyt Funeral Home was in charge of arrangements.

The deceased had no known rel- atives. He was a bachelor and lived by himself.

MRS. MARY BALL DIES AT HOSPITAL

Mrs. Mary Ball, 13338 Baltimore ave., passed away at a hospital af- ter a lingering illness of long dur- ation on Thursday, Jan. 4. She was 70 years of age at the time of her death.

Pfc. Cas. Pawlak Has Close Shave With China Reds

With the U. S. Second Infantry Division in Korea.—Pfc. Casimir Pawlak, Jr., son of Mrs. Mary Pawlak, 3214 E. 133rd st. (Hege- wisch), started through a Chinese communist trap in the Kunu-ri Pass in a jeep, but had to abandon it in favor of another vehicle.

"Just like in the movies," Paw- lak reported to his commanding officer. "The Chinese shot out our gas tank. Luckily for me, there was another truck just ahead that didn't have a driver."

Pawlak and the other occupants boarded the standing vehicle, a ¾ ton truck.

"As soon as we got started again," continued Pawlak, "we began loading wounded soldiers on the truck. We used what first aid equipment we had for the wounded men and by the grace of God were able to bring them all into a collecting station for initial treatment."

At the conclusion of the hectic trip through the pass, their newly acquired vehicle showed not a single mark to testify to the sav- ageness of the Chinese trap.

MRS. MARY SOWA DIES AT A\ E 75

Battle of Ballots Looms Near; Lineup in 9th and 10th Wards

With primary day still a month and a half away the political pot is already bubbling merrily away with the only concern—in one ward, at least—about suficient candidates.

Reginald DuBois vs. Henry Vree in the 9th ward.

Emil V. Pacini vs. the field in the 10th ward.

That's the way things stack up at the present time. With seven of Hegewisch's nine precincts within the 9th ward, perhaps that fight should be the most interest- ing, but all of Hegewisch will ob- serve with interest and two pre- cincts will participate in the cat- and-dog fight shaping up in the 10th ward.

Reginald DuBois, present alder- man of the 9th ward, will run for re-election. He will file his peti- tion this morning (Friday). Mr. DuBois has an outstanding record in the city council, having a per-

fect attendance record at cour meetings for the past five ye and a perfect attendance reco for attending committee and s he is a member for the past fe years. Such representation of ward by an alderman is virtua unknown in this day of indiff ence.

DuBois' Opponent'

Running against Alderman I Bosi is a politician unknown, H ry Vree, who owns and operate butcher and grocery shop on 11 st. Vree was endorsed by the ward regular Democratic orga zation by resolution January 1951, (see text of resolution on side pages) after a search of organization revealed no prosp tive candidate. Mr. Vree has be active in civic affairs as chairm of the mayor's committee for cleaner Chicago for the Kensi ton-Roseland area, in the Lie club, as a director of the Rosela School of Christian Instruct and other organizations.

In the 10th ward, Emil V. Pac is a candidate for re-election alderman of the ward. He is present Democratic committee

---

Once the Office of Civilian Defense was disbanded in 1945, the *News Weekly* reverted to civilian proprietorship under new owners Emily Lindberg, Irene Stancik, and Harry Jacobsen. Their partnership ended in tragedy, however, when Jacobsen was killed in an airplane accident at the Lansing Airport in 1946. Lindberg and Stancik sold the paper to Gene Czachorski. While Lindberg devoted herself to family matters, Stancik joined the Foreign Service. Czachorski was the son of Dr. John Czachorski and attorney Helen (Fleming) Czachorski. He and his brother John grew up in Hegewisch, and both became lawyers. Prior to the war, he had been one of the founders of the Hegewisch Community Committee. He practiced law in Chicago and quietly dedicated the *Hegewisch News* to promoting Hegewisch's cause at city hall and to highlighting the good things that Hegewisch adults and youth did for the community. He married another Hegewisch native, Violet Tukich, and became an enthusiastic homeowner and parent in the 1950s, often describing his attempts at gardening and remodeling in his From the Editor's Scratchpad column. (Author's collection.)

Postwar, public works projects resumed around Hegewisch. First, the State of Illinois designated the Illinois side of Wolf Lake as a state conservation park in the fall of 1946. Then the new 130th Street bridge over the Calumet River was opened as part of the Illinois Waterway project in 1949. The 1939 proposed Lake Calumet Airport was now a dead issue. Its 300-acre site had become a Municipal Sanitary Landfill with trucks and trains dumping about 1,800 cubic yards of refuse daily into the north end of Lake Calumet. Other nearby dump sites were at Republic Steel, General Chemical, and the Calumet River Turning Basin 5 at 130th Street. All contained household and construction refuse plus various industrial toxins. The Water Pollution Control Act of 1948 gave Illinois and Chicago the authority to implement pollution control ordinances and laws, but industries continued to ignore the problem. In 1949, landfills were considered an efficient and sensible method for the containment of all types of waste, although no one knew if leachates might harm ground water or the natural environment. (Both, SCHM.)

Six

HEGEWISCH AT MID-CENTURY

With a new editor, the *Hegewisch News* began to push to get improvements for Hegewisch. Editorials also highlighted returning GIs and home life and constantly encouraged people to "shop local." Among the improvements achieved were a weekly visit from the Chicago Public Library's bookmobile, the opening of the K-channel off Wolf Lake, and the connecting of Lake Calumet Harbor with the St. Lawrence Seaway. Still, the park district denied a swimming pool for Mann Park.

New houses went up in Arizona and behind the park to offset the postwar housing shortage. Yet prairies and marshes still separated Hegewisch from the rest of the city, and residents still felt isolated, and city hall still had trouble recognizing the neighborhood as a part of Chicago. In fact, Hegewisch was sometimes described as a "rural community" because of its prairies and bodies of water.

A big event was the visit in 1950 of the nephew of the town's namesake, Adolf Hegewisch, some 70 years after his uncle brought him to see the factory being erected. Churches and schools were built, and the US government installed one of its Nike Ajax sites on the shore of Wolf Lake.

All of these things took place while Pressed Steel Car struggled to stay profitable with innovative products until it changed its name and sold the Hegewisch property to US Steel-Supply.

In August 1950, Adolph Hegewisch (center), nephew of *the* Adolf Hegewisch, visited the town that was named for his uncle. He is shown shaking hands with *Hegewisch News* editor/publisher Gene Czachorski in front of the Pressed Steel Car office building. To his right is Perry Hallberg. The last time young Adolf visited was in 1884 when he accompanied his uncle to the USRSC construction site. (SCHM.)

A mainstay of the *Hegewisch News* was Helen Hwastecki. A native Hegewischite, she wrote the About People column throughout the 1950s and 1960s. Her weekly feature included items about church suppers, newcomers, births, boys in the military, Foreign Service postings, and wedding showers. Emily Lindberg wrote an occasional column called Mind's Eye View, which described significant events in greater detail. (Author's collection.)

The "Mann Park swimming pool" was a standard joke in Hegewisch by 1950 when the park board once again denied the neighborhood a swimming pool. Since the 1930s, the Chamber of Commerce had argued that Hegewisch was four miles away from the closest pool. Mann Park on the northwest side was almost a mile away from residents on the southeast side with a railroad track in between, adding to the hazards of the trip. Children swam in Wolf Lake or in the abandoned railroad water towers in the prairie north of 133rd Street, which everyone called "The Tanks." Mann Park, occupying four square blocks, contained one of the smallest field houses in the city, a sand box, a few swings, a slide, a few tennis courts, and no ice rink judging by this photograph of Betty Pobereyko skating on a puddle. When the board said its $24 million bond issue had to be used "on the basis of need," the *Hegewisch News* asked, "What, in the name of all that is good, constitutes 'need' in your eyes?" (Janet Sharko.)

People were in the mood to party when the war ended, and part of the fun included local taverns, which threw New Year's Eve parties and Friday fish fries. Many of the taverns started as saloons in early Hegewisch, like Joe's, the South Shore Inn, Beacon, and Krupa's in Arizona. Fleischman's went a little upscale with its new owners calling it the Colonial Club. Joe's was operated by Joe Pavich Jr. for a time, and he was a founding member of the South Chicago Tavern Owners Association. Wojtas's and Forystek's continued to have bar service as well as a hall for wedding receptions and funeral luncheons. A couple of new taverns joined the scene. Blondie's run by Mike "Ace" and Stephanie (Krupa) Pobereyko took over the former Hegewisch State Bank Building on Brandon Avenue. Pete and Wanda Pobereyko ran the packaged liquor end of things. Club 505 opened on Brainard Avenue in the late 1940s and for decades afterward was known throughout the Calumet Region for its polka parties and radio broadcasts. (Author's collection.)

Milan's Snack Shop (above) at 13301 Baltimore Avenue, owned by Sam Panayotovich, was one of the first eateries in Hegewisch to serve pizza. The Opera House Buffet had opened there in 1888, followed by the Wachowiak Brothers restaurant and confectionery shop of the 1920s and 1930s. In the 1940s, it became Cozy Corner, where "bobby soxers" gathered around the jukebox to dance. (SCHM.)

Some called it a variety shop because the Milky Way stocked a wide range of items from ice cream and soft drinks to toys, books, and over-the-counter drugs. Operated by Emma Paprochi at 13322 Baltimore Avenue, next door to the theater, it also had a soda fountain. In the 1930s, Emma and her husband, Henry, ran the Meadowmoor Dairy at 13350 Baltimore Avenue. (SCHM.)

Along with returning GIs came weddings and babies. Above are Jimmy Ostrom (left) and his cousin Bettianne Pobereyko, both born in 1946 at the very beginning of the national baby boom during which approximately 79 million people were born. These new Hegewisch families often made their first homes in apartments or with grandparents due to a nationwide housing shortage. (Janet Sharko.)

Paging through *Soups, Salads 'n Vegetables* makes the reader long for 1950s comfort food. Produced by the PTA of St. Florian School in 1952, the cookbook was a fundraiser and is now a record of what Hegewisch families enjoyed at mealtime. A few examples are *kukietka*, *paczki* (Polish bismarks), *gaty* (stuffed potato balls), Polish sausage, stuffed cabbage, veal roast with sour cream and mushroom gravy, and babka. (Author's collection.)

In the spring of 1950, one solution to the postwar housing problem in Hegewisch was Island Park Trailer Court at 13240 Avenue F. The developer, James J. Haines, was president of Cinders Inc. and known for his support of Lake Calumet Harbor. William J. McDillon, president of the East Side Chamber of Commerce and the Calumet Region Congress, was general manager of the park. As a means of including the newcomers, the *Hegewisch News* began a column called Island Park News written by Mildred Mabry. She noted the comings and goings of residents, holiday events, and the interesting people who called the park home. Executives and military who were transferred to the Chicago area brought their own trailers and lived next door to musicians like the Beaver Valley Sweethearts who appeared on WLS Radio's *National Barn Dance* or down the street from Clinton Twiss, author of *The Long Long Trailer*, later a movie starring Lucille Ball and Desi Arnaz. The original trailers were long gone by the turn of the 20th century and replaced by manufactured homes (above.). (Author's collection.)

Out of envy, perhaps, or inside knowledge, the subdivision of houses that was built on the north end of Arizona in the early 1950s was sometimes called West Mortgage Heights. Located between 133rd and 132nd Streets, from Avenue N to Avenue L, these modest single-family brick houses undoubtedly raised eyebrows among Arizona old-timers who still lived in frame houses dating back to World War I or before. (Author's collection.)

In anticipation of a surge of young people needing education, the parish of St. Columba began raising money to build a school and a new church. Part of the fundraising program was holding a carnival every summer, which included rides and refreshments. By the fall of 1950, the land had been purchased and the cornerstone laid in April 1951. (SCHM.)

Reverend Thomas J. Kelly, pastor of St. Columba, was key in completing the combination church and school building project. Needed next were teachers, for which he turned to the Sisters of St. Benedict at Nauvoo, Illinois. They agreed to staff the new school (at right) and welcomed 160 pupils to the first session in September 1951. Hegewisch now had two parochial schools and one public elementary school. (SCHM.)

In 1940, St. Hedwig Polish National Catholic Church was organized as a community-based church that initially held services in the Opera House with the Reverend Grabek as pastor. The cornerstone for the church at 3320 East 134th Street was laid in 1949. (SCHM.)

Hegewisch had always had a lot of clubs. In the 1920s and 1930s they tended to be for young adults as social venues or athletic groups. After World War II, there were activities for younger people sponsored by the park district and the Hegewisch Community Committee. Some of the churches sponsored Girl and Boy Scout troops. Little League and Babe Ruth League teams soon followed, while the Polish Alma Mater Drum and Bugle Corps kept up its work until later groups such as the Hegewisch Raiders and the Illiana Lancers superseded it. Among the adults there were always church groups to participate in. Club Limonowa, sponsored by St. Florian, was devoted to aiding victims of the war in Poland. The schools all had PTAs. The Federation of Lodges was an umbrella group formed by Frank Sowa to help Hegewisch achieve the improvements that it needed and paid for with its taxes. (SCHM.)

During the 1950s, the Cold War was always an American concern. In 1955, the government installed Nike Ajax surface-to-air missiles on the north side of Wolf Lake as part of Project Nike. Located in Chicago-Gary Defense Area C, Hegewisch was site 44. The 20 bases of the Chicago area came under the Fifth Army Air Defense Command with early coordination of area air defenses originating at a "Missile Master" facility at Arlington Heights. It was rumored that some of the Hegewisch batteries carried nuclear warheads, but they were never upgraded to the Nike Hercules nuclear version. Locals remember the exercises on Saturday afternoons when the missiles rose up from their launch pads and rotated in a practice session. The Air Force, critical of the Army's Nike system, conducted a mock attack against Chicago in 1958 to discredit Nike effectiveness. Nike Ajax did not fare well. The Hegewisch/Wolf Lake site was decommissioned in March 1963. The buildings were razed, but the foundations remain. Pictured above is 1st Lt. John M. Hyde III, a member of the last unit at this site. (SCHM.)

The Southeast Sportsmen's Club (SES) was organized in the East Side neighborhood in 1934 with the purpose of conservation, restoration, and improvement of Wolf Lake and other local natural resources. Its members were also avid hunters and fishermen, using fox hunts as shown above, for instance, to protect rabbits and pheasants. Besides club news, the SES newsletter reported on oil dumped in Indian Creek and numerous sick and dying birds along the northern shore of Lake Calumet in 1955. However, the club's mettle was tested in 1956 after it had moved to Hegewisch when the Gary (Indiana) Chamber of Commerce proposed that 130th Street be extended eastward from Lake Calumet Harbor through Hegewisch and Wolf Lake to Indiana. While the Chicago Port Authority and State of Indiana thought this was a splendid idea, the residents of Hegewisch opposed it because 130th Street would then become a state arterial highway with limited access and an expected 8,000 vehicles per day coming through. The SES contended that the necessary causeway would destroy Wolf Lake. The proposal finally died in 1960. (SCHM.)

The clubhouse (above) at 13139 South Avenue M was dedicated in June 1955. During the opening event, James Haines, president of Island Park Homes; Sen. Walker Butler; and others were given honorary memberships. The clubhouse included a 325-foot harbor and a house for the caretaker, Edward Shumaker. That same year, the Shedd Estate donated a tract of land on the east side of today's K-channel (below) to the Illinois Department of Conservation. Several private property owners at the south end of the lake also donated land, while the SES, the Wolf Lake Rod & Gun Club, and others each donated 50-foot parcels on the west side. Dredging began in 1956, resulting in a channel that opened the lake to 132nd Street for public use in time for ice fishing in the winter of 1957. (Above, SCHM; below, author's collection.)

In June 1945, when the last Sherman M4A1 tanks rolled off the line, ending their production, at Hegewisch, 3,100 workers were laid off. Shortly afterward, PSC announced plans to begin producing domestic appliances. In November, the new household appliance division showed off its prototype electric range called Presteline. It was innovative because the purchaser had the option of a model with all four burners arranged in a line at the back of the range—out of reach of children's hands. Production got underway in 1946. Plans also called for the production of refrigerators, water heaters, kitchen cabinets, automatic clothes washers, and dryers in Hegewisch. However, in 1948, the Admiral Corporation purchased the household appliance division. PSC continued to produce freight cars at its plant in Mount Vernon, Illinois, and to acquire many smaller metal manufacturers. Then in January 1951, it picked up an Army contract to process combat vehicles at the Hegewisch plant, preparing them for use or storage. (Author's collection.)

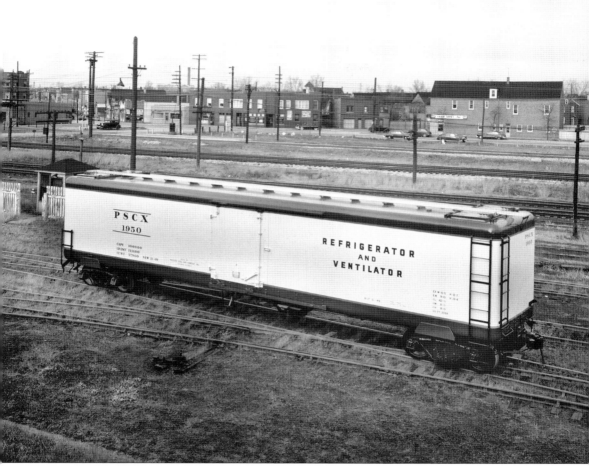

In trying to stabilize its business during a steel shortage, PSC announced a new freight car in 1950. Designed by Bertrand Goldberg, the Unicel was a one-piece structure of molded plywood. Its only metal parts were couplers, draft gear, trucks, grab irons, and door frames. The ends, sides, roof, and floor of the car (shown here with Hegewisch in the background) were made of cross-laminated plywood faces bonded to laminated wood cores at the ends; to wood ribbing at the roof and sides; and to a cellular structure at the floor. A Unicel offered 23 percent more capacity than the same size steel car, was 15,000 pounds lighter, and cost 17 percent less to build. Despite approval by the Association of American Railroads, officials of the railroads themselves could not be convinced, and it never went into production. PSC continued to acquire smaller metalworking companies. The Mount Vernon car plant closed for good in 1954, the same year in which the company changed its name to United States Industries Inc. The United States Steel Supply Division purchased the Hegewisch property in 1956. (HB-12829-B Chicago History Museum Hedrich Blessing Collection.)

During the boom years of the 1950s, Cargill expanded its operation on the Calumet River, near 122nd Street. Graycor, founded in 1922 as the Chicago Concrete Breaking Co., opened its new 26-acre site at 12233 Avenue O in October 1952. Mainstays of the community were businesses like Iron and Steel Products at 13500 Brainard Avenue, which had occupied the old Ryan Car site since the late 1930s. (SCHM.)

Riding the wave of the Illinois Waterway development of the 1950s, Hegewisch Lumber at 13651 South Buffalo Avenue changed its name to Calumet Harbor Lumber. The company had been in business at this site since 1922, and it was still owned and operated by the Beckman family. It is known today for being the only sawmill in the city of Chicago. (SCHM.)

Sand for the construction of the Indiana Toll Road and the Chicago Skyway in the 1950s was dug from a borrow pit roughly a mile south of Wolf Lake. The pit eventually filled with water and was named Powderhorn Lake. A state nature preserve, Powderhorn occupies a 35-acre remnant of the dune-and-swale topography on which Hegewisch was built. It opened for fishing in 1960. (SCHM.)

A Chicago native, Walker Butler was a champion of the southeast side in its quest for completion of the Illinois Waterway. He was often called the "Father of Lake Calumet Harbor" and the "Father of Wolf Lake." Between 1943 and 1953, he served in the Illinois Senate and finished his career in 1969 as a Cook County Circuit Court judge. (Author's collection.)

Located at the junction of 130th Street, the Lakes-to-Gulf Waterway, and the Calumet Expressway, Lake Calumet Harbor connected Hegewisch to the world in 1957 once the St. Lawrence Seaway was completed. In the upper right of the photograph is the O'Brien Lock and Dam on the Calumet River; Hegewisch is in the upper left. Butler Drive, named for Walker Butler, parallels the dock. (Michael Aniol.)

Work began on Lake Calumet Harbor the day after the proceeds from a $25 million bond issue were turned over to the Chicago Port District in 1955. New warehouses were built, and a fourth overseas shipping company contracted for port facilities at the Calumet Harbor Terminals Inc. The grain elevators constructed at that time were impressive and can still handle 14 million bushels of grain. (Author's collection.)

Seven

HOMETOWN ACTIVISM

The final piece of the Lakes-to-Gulf Waterway was put in place in the early 1960s with the construction of the O'Brien Lock and Dam just west of Hegewisch. The last big subdivision, Avalon Trails, was built out north of the original town, and after some years of dealing with the Chicago school board, the neighborhood also had its own elementary school.

Equally successful was the *Hegewisch News*'s pitch to the Chicago Public Library board to give the neighborhood a better library than a weekly bookmobile. The *Hegewisch News* was also on top of things with regard to snow removal, especially in the aftermath of the historic Blizzard of 1967, which paralyzed the entire city and isolated Hegewisch more than ever.

The fact that Hegewisch was separated from heavy industry only by a river, some marshland, and railroads made it vulnerable to air and water pollution. These generally became important issues in the 1960s, but the *Hegewisch News* took a leadership role on the matter in the 1970s, urging the city to dump its refuse somewhere else.

The above photograph depicts the Thomas J. O'Brien Lock and Dam under construction. It was the final piece in the Lakes-to-Gulf Waterway and was in place by1960, although the St. Lawrence Seaway had opened in 1957. The largest lock in the system, it is located south of 130th Street on the Calumet River. The St. Lawrence Seaway ends in the middle where the Illinois Waterway begins. The lock and dam are used to maintain a nine-foot draft and to mitigate unusual flood conditions that could take too much water from Lake Michigan or send too much storm water into the lake. Also seen in the photograph below is Hegewisch Marsh (the trees in the lower half). Across the river is the property that became the subject of landfill protests in Hegewisch during the 1970s. (Both, SCHM.)

Built north of 130th Street amongst railroad tracks, industrial sites, and landfill operations, Avalon Trails was originally platted as Ford City Subdivision 2. In 1960, a new builder renamed it Avalon Trails. By 1965, there were 600 families in residence who understood that they lived in Hegewisch, but that Avalon Trails was located in another ward and its civic problems were different. (Author's collection.)

NEWSLETTER STAFF

E. Borowski
B. Michalski
G. Michalski
K. Rhodes
L. Zahrn

Phone: 646-1108

AVALON TRAILS IMPROVEMENT ASSOCIATION

NEWSLETTER

EDITOR: JIM FINLAYSON

12915 SOUTH CARONDOLET AVENUE ● CHICAGO, ILLINOIS 60633

VOLUME 9   NUMBER 5

A.T.I.A. MEETING

The regular monthly meeting of the Avalon Trails Improvement Association will be held at the Sutka VFW Post #5414, 13301 South Brainard on Thursday June 3, 1971, at 8 p.m. sharp. Try to attend and bring a friend. Everyone is invited--whether a member or not.

PICNIC TIME

ATIA Annual Picnic will be on Sunday August 1, 1 at Eggers Woods, 112th and Avenue B. We are ing to get a little head start this year and trying to get more help--please fill out the

130th STREET AND PUBLIC ROADS COMMITTEE

This community is being entertained with a game of "Pass the Buck" by the Street and Sanitation Department of our City.

On April 6, 1971, in a communication to that department, this organization expressed its delight while examining campaign brochures for Mayor Daley. In them we found under a subtitle of "things to come in the near future" the widening and asphalt resurfacing of 130th Street from Saginaw Avenue to Brandon Avenue. We registered an inquiry as to the width of the street and the time schedule of when this improvement can be expected.

In a reply we received a letter dated April 26, 1971 from Commissioner James J McDonough and co-signed by Deputy Commissioner Michael Robinson. We will reprint the one paragraph relating to the

In 1962, the neighborhood organized the Avalon Trails Improvement Association. The following year, they had a charter and a monthly newsletter that addressed issues of concern such as a proposed railroad embankment cutting the subdivision in two, the 130th Street extension, landfills and dumping, obtaining a proper library, the Torrence Avenue and 130th Street intersection, and the need for an elementary school. (Author's collection.)

As the Lakes-to-Gulf Waterway took shape in the 1950s, the Army Corps of Engineers revisited the Calumet River, determining that bridge clearance must be 200 feet horizontally and 21 feet vertically in the closed position. The existing Chicago & Western Indiana Railroad bridge did not pass, but it was not until 1967 and after the Avalon Trails subdivision was built out that the bridge, located several blocks north, was scheduled for replacement. A new southern approach for the Calumet & Western Railway, which would share the new bridge, required an embankment to run northwest from Muskegon Avenue and 127th Street to just north of 126th Street and Saginaw Avenue. This earthwork cutting through the northwest quadrant of Avalon Trails meant the condemnation of four brand new houses and placement of railroad tracks within 30 feet of many others. So incensed were Avalon Trails homeowners that they took their grievance all the way to the office of Pres. Lyndon B. Johnson. Even so, they lost their case. Some of the remaining houses can be seen to the left. (Author's collection.)

In December 1967, the Avalon Trails Improvement Association school committee attended its fifth Chicago Board of Education meeting to present its request for a local school. There were 727 families in the neighborhood with 1,435 children and another 135 houses under construction. Afterward, the board announced a September 1969 move-in date for the Virgil Grissom Public School at 128th Street and Escanaba Avenue in the heart of Avalon Trails. (SCHM.)

Talk about a high school for the East Side and Hegewisch started in the late 1940s. Hegewisch boosters tried hard to convince the school board that Hegewisch was the ideal place for it and that the best name for it would be Wilson Frankland, a well-known southeast side labor and education leader. In the end, it opened in 1956 in the East Side and was named George Washington High School. (SCHM.)

In the late winter of 1965, ground was broken for a new educational complex at St. Florian. By November, a new classroom building, gym, and cafeteria were in place as well as a new convent and chapel for the Franciscan Sisters of Chicago who taught at the school. (SCHM.)

In 1958, Lebanon Lutheran Church was scheduled to be closed because it had never outgrown its mission status. However, about this time, the Avalon Trails subdivision opened, and the parish gained a significant number of new members—enough so that by 1969, the cornerstone was laid for a brand new church (above) at 13100 Manistee Avenue. The first services were held there in March 1970. (SCHM.)

The year 1960 was a banner one for improvements in Hegewisch. During the 1950s, the *Hegewisch News* had lobbied the Chicago Public Library (CPL) for a proper library, while residents collected signatures on petitions. The Hegewisch CPL branch was still operating out of a corner of Rzonca's "library store" on Baltimore Avenue, which was far from helpful to students who had to do research and read certain books. The CPL's reluctant solution was a bookmobile in 1958 that parked on Baltimore Avenue every Tuesday to dispense books and take orders for the next delivery. Finally, the neighborhood convinced the library board that they were worthy of a real library in a real building. The Hegewisch Branch opened at 13445 Brandon Avenue in May 1960. Next, a swimming pool for Mann Park opened on July 1. The pool had been promised since at least 1932, the year the field house was opened. To cap off the year, in November a new post office opened at 13234 Baltimore Avenue. (SCHM.)

The historic Blizzard of 1967 took everyone in Chicago by surprise. The scenes here are 133rd Street between Avenues N and M (above) and the side yard of 13315 Avenue N in the aftermath of the January 26–27 storm. The *Hegewisch News* reported a spirit of friendliness and helpfulness in Hegewisch mixed with bitterness toward the city because of its poor snow removal performance. While roads were blocked, the Chicago Fire Department's helicopter came four times to rescue those in trouble. Republic Steel sent plows, which opened main streets within a day or so, while the city plows did not arrive until Sunday. The following week another 12.5 inches fell. The *Hegewisch News* joined many other newspapers across the city in demanding better service in the future. (Both, Alex Skalka family.)

Army Specialist Carmel B. Harvey Jr. of the 1st Calvary Division served as a fire team leader in Vietnam's Binh Dinh Province. It was reported that during a firefight on June 21, 1967, two members of his squad were wounded. Suddenly, an enemy bullet hit and activated the fuse on a hand grenade attached to Harvey's belt. Unable to remove it and realizing the danger to his comrades if he remained with them, he jumped to his feet, shouted a challenge at the enemy and raced toward them. He had nearly reached the enemy position when the grenade exploded, killing him and momentarily stunning the enemy machine gun crew. The pause in enemy fire allowed the wounded men to be moved to safety. For his action, Harvey was awarded the Congressional Medal of Honor and the Purple Heart. At home, Olive-Harvey College is named for him and fellow Medal of Honor recipient Milton L. Olive III. The auditorium of George Washington High School, his alma mater, has been named Harvey Hall. (SCHM.)

Hegewisch News lost its longtime editor and publisher in 1971 when Gene Czachorski passed away. Towards the end, he asked his wife, Violet (Tukich) Czarchorski, to keep the paper going. At first, she was reluctant, but as the environmental issues concerning Hegewisch piled up during the 1970s, she took control and became a leader in several movements created to save Hegewisch from destruction. She had grown up in Hegewisch and, in the 1940s, earned a bachelor's degree in dietary science from Illinois Institute of Technology. In 1945, she wrote a column for the *News Weekly* called Kitchen Korner. Later, she earned a master's degree in library science. As editor and publisher of *Hegewisch News*, she wrote editorial after editorial describing the ways in which refuse and toxic waste disposal companies were adding to the pollution of local land and waterways. She also participated in protests and rallies that eventually resulted in more government oversight of land use in the area. Violet Czachorski published the *Hegewisch News* for 17 years, retiring in 1988. (Author's collection.)

Hegewisch was built on the slopes and swales of the Lake Michigan Plain. It had no natural "highlands" like the one above on the Little Calumet River, which resulted from solid waste landfills. With Clean Air and Water Acts passed by Congress in 1973, beginning in 1978, Hegewisch resisted Chicago's attempts to turn the neighborhood and surrounding wetlands into the city dump. (Author's collection.)

The *Hegewisch News*, Avalon Trails Improvement Association, and others protested the landfill operations of Heil (a wetland at 131st Street and Torrence Avenue), Calumet Industrial Disposal (1634–1998 134th Street and 138th Street and the Calumet Expressway), Hyon (138th Street and Doty Avenue), and Calumet Incinerator (Chicago's solid waste dump at the north end of Lake Calumet since 1939). Chemical Waste Management was potentially turning the shores of Lake Calumet into a toxic quagmire. (Author's collection.)

Occasionally called "Mt. Trashmore," Paxton II (above) is 170 feet tall and covers 58 acres in a wetland area less than a mile from Lake Calumet. One of the worst sinners was Calumet Container, which straddled the Indiana state line on 134th Street, 200 yards north of Powderhorn Lake, while processing drums of industrial chemicals between 1960 and 1980. Shuttered in 1980, its soil was removed in 1984. (Author's collection.)

Under protest, Waste Management/CID attempted to create landfills along the O'Brien Lock and Dam. Above, Lake Calumet is seen from Paxton II. Out of sight to the left is a "cluster site" of four highly toxic dumps, which are still being monitored. While the protesters could not stop landfills from operating, they did ensure that haphazard use of wetlands for garbage disposal was a thing of the past. (Author's collection.)

Eight

COMING FULL CIRCLE

July 9–11, 1983, was the culmination of a year of reminiscing about the history of Hegewisch and its people. The *Hegewisch News* ran a year-long series on businesses and events from the 1880s to the present, including excerpts from its predecessor the *Hegewisch News Weekly*. For three days in July, the town celebrated with a parade, street dancing, and a dinner party.

Then the news went back to current events such as the ongoing opposition to landfills ringing the neighborhood. In the late 1980s, US Steel closed its supply warehouse on Torrence Avenue in Hegewisch. Members of the Avalon Trails Improvement Association (ATIA) formed a committee to seek a new library for Hegewisch, which was successful. However, on the heels of its ribbon cutting ceremony was the city's announcement that it was proposing to place an airport on top of Hegewisch.

Then, as suddenly as the threat had appeared, it went away. By 1994, Hegewisch was back to normal. Its newspaper had changed hands three times, and it now had a brand new Chicago South Shore & South Bend Railroad station plus a wetland preserve called Hegewisch Marsh on land that had been threatened with use as a landfill. Two environmental preservation organizations now made their homes in Hegewisch.

In the following 20 years, the intersection of 130th Street, Torrence Avenue, and Brainard Avenue was reconfigured and featured a depressed roadway, something the ATIA and others in Hegewisch had recommended in the 1960s. And the old USRSC/PSC/US Steel property was sold to a company that would manufacture, of all things, railcars.

Hegewisch had come full circle.

Preceded by a year of reminiscing about early Hegewisch, the big weekend arrived when Hegewisch celebrated its 100th anniversary from July 9 through July 11, 1983. Street dancing accompanied by the Pala Brothers orchestra drew big crowds. A local television station recorded the events. The parade on Saturday featured Miss Hegewisch, Marlene Mitchell, along with veterans groups, Scouts, costumed Polish dancers, politicians, police on horseback, and floats from businesses near and far. Local celebrity Mary "Kid Montana" Koulentiky waved to the crowds from her horse-drawn carriage while nonprofit groups like the Lions Club manned refreshment stands along Baltimore Avenue. A variety show and a centennial dinner capped the weekend. With this success in mind, the neighborhood hosted its annual Hegewisch-Fest each summer. (Both, SCHM.)

Hegewisch resident Ed Blaszak was the designer of the Republic Steel monument in 1981, his theme being the relationship of the steel industry (the six tall uprights) with the people of the southeast side (the base). The four short uprights represent the four surrounding communities. Blaszak, a 21-year employee of the company, had studied art and design at the Art Institute of Chicago. The monument was constructed with local steel. (SCHM.)

Hegewisch's third Chicago South Shore & South Bend (CSS&SB) passenger station was completed in 1992. With a Craftsman-style look, it was located about three blocks southeast of the original one on Brainard Avenue. Michael A. Shymanski, AIA emeritus of the Pullman neighborhood of Chicago, was the architect. With the new station, the parking lot was expanded to the west, and another lot across the street on Avenue O was added. (Author's collection.)

The HERALD

The South Chicago HERALD

After Vi Czachorski retired and sold the *Hegewisch News* in 1988, she continued to report on environmental issues for a few more weeks. The new editor and publisher was Al Bodie. The following year, he sold to John R. Casey, who added *East Side News* to the masthead. Society columnist Helen Hwastecki continued to produce her weekly column. In October 1990, a new set of publishers, Lee H. Anglin and George Grbic, took over with Janet Hughes as general manager. They changed the name to the *Hegewisch Herald*, but it became the *Herald* in January 1993, which served the communities of Hegewisch, East Side, South Chicago, Burnham, and Calumet City, the latter two being suburbs of Chicago. For the next year, the publication belonged to Lakeview Publishing, until it changed hands in early 1994, becoming part of the Sunset News Group with Janet (Hughes) Anglin as publisher and Jane Hopkins as editor. Sunset changed the name to the *South Chicago Herald*, thus ending a 58-year run as Hegewisch's own neighborhood newspaper. (SCHM.)

By the late 1970s, the Hegewisch Branch of the Chicago Public Library was outgrowing its space. In the mid-1980s, the Avalon Trails Improvement Association formed a Library Committee with neighborhood resident Judith Lihota as its chair. Circulation statistics were gathered and presented to Hegewisch's representative in Springfield in a bid for funding. In the spring of 1989, a building site was procured and groundbreaking took place in November with Mayor Richard M. Daley on hand for the ceremony. The following spring, construction was underway. The new 12,000-square-foot Hegewisch Library at 130th Street and Houston Avenue opened in December 1991. With over 40,000 books, the collection was now three times bigger than at the Brandon Avenue location. Pictured are, from left to right, state representative Sam Panayotovich, Library Committee chair Judith Lihota, unidentified, head librarian Paul Bollheimer, unidentified, Alderman John Buchanan, and unidentified. (Both, SCHM.)

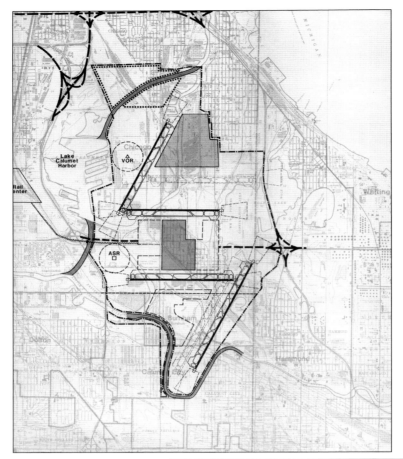

In November 1989, Mayor Richard M. Daley appeared in Hegewisch to witness the groundbreaking for its new library. On February 15, 1990, he announced his proposal for the Lake Calumet Airport, which would entail the complete leveling of Hegewisch (the gray L-shaped box at center) and would drastically alter the natural environment of the southeast side. (Author's collection.)

Protesters organized throughout the southeast side, Burnham, and Calumet City—all of which would be affected by the proposed airport's "footprint." As the months went by, local leaders cautioned against panic selling of homes. They said that even though the mayor had made a deal with the governor, they would still have to convince the Environmental Protection Agency, the Federal Aviation Administration, and the Army Corps of Engineers before implementation. (SCHM.)

Accused of arrogance, the mayor justified demolishing a neighborhood with promises of jobs for residents and containment of polluted land with airport runways. He did not address the fate of existing businesses and their employees. Homeowners argued that "fair market value" would not cover the cost of buying a comparable house elsewhere. Environmentalists feared how the destruction of wetlands would adversely affect the ecology. The T-shirt at right began appearing around town. (Author's collection.)

THE CITIZENS AGAINST THE LAKE CALUMET AIRPORT (C.A.L.C.A.) WILL HOLD A VERY IMPORTANT MEETING. DATE: THURS. JULY 26th TIME: 7:00 P.M. SHARP PLACE: MANN PARK FIELDHOUSE YOU HAVE HEARD THE LIES NOW COME AND HEAR THE TRUTH! SAVE YOUR HOME SAVE YOUR COMMUNITY SAVE YOUR CHURCHES

In July 1992, almost as stealthily as it appeared, the third airport idea disappeared. It could have been Democrat versus Republican politics, state versus city politics, lack of interest by the airlines, disinterest at the federal level, exorbitant cost, or perhaps the will of the people who would have been most affected by it. Mayor Daley walked away from a Lake Calumet Airport, and Hegewisch breathed easier. (Author's collection.)

The opposition to garbage and toxic waste disposal around Hegewisch and Lake Calumet continued in the 1980s and 1990s. In 1989, the Southeast Environmental Task Force (SETF) was organized by Marian Byrnes as a coalition of 30 organizations intent on counteracting the construction of a garbage incinerator on the former Wisconsin Steel site (106th Street and Torrence Avenue). Its office was and is still located at 13300 Baltimore Avenue, the former Klucker's Pharmacy building. During those years, the 129 acres of wetlands at 131st Street and Torrence Avenue that had been threatened with destruction by the E.F. Heil Company was preserved as the Hegewisch Marsh. The west side of the marsh (above) can be seen from the O'Brien lock. A haven for wetland birds and plants (left), it is owned by the Chicago Park District (Both, author's collection.)

A contemporary of SETF was the Calumet Ecological Park Association (CEPA) founded in 1993 by Dr. James Landing (second from right) to promote the idea of an ecological park within the Calumet Region. The National Park Service authored a feasibility study in 1998 that suggested designation as a National Heritage Area, which led to the founding of the Calumet Heritage Partnership to facilitate its development. (SCHM.)

Since 1994, the intersection of Torrence Avenue, 130th Street, Brainard Avenue, and the defunct CWI railroad has been reconfigured. 130th Street in Avalon Trails dead ends at Brainard Avenue, which now connects Indiana truck routes to Torrence Avenue then becomes 130th Street on the west side of it. Southbound Torrence Avenue slips beneath the CSS&SB and the Norfolk & Western tracks (as ATIA suggested in the 1960s), and the CSS&SB has a new bridge. (Author's collection.)

Draped with wild vines, the remains of the Pressed Steel Car gate remind people that the more things change, the more they stay the same. On the land behind that gate, near the intersection of Brandon and Brainard Avenues, USRSC began a tradition of building railcars in Hegewisch, which has come full circle with the opening of CRRC Sinfang America at 13535 South Torrence Avenue. USRSC was the child of British investors; CRRC comes out of a German company founded in China between 1900 and 1902. The Illinois-based subsidiary of CRRC Corporation Ltd. is headquartered in Chicago. Its business is to design, engineer, and manufacture passenger rail vehicles and high-speed trains. The contract with the Chicago Transit Authority (CTA) for the 7000 Series cars, which provides the CTA with new rolling stock for the first time in 50 years, was signed in 2016. Groundbreaking took place in March 2017, and the factory was in full operation the summer of 2019. (Above, author's collection; below, CRRC.)

BIBLIOGRAPHY

Abstract of title to the property at 13259 South Baltimore Avenue, Chicago, Illinois

Ancestry.com

Colten, Craig E. *Industrial Wastes in the Calumet Area, 1869–1970, An Historical Geography.* Champaign, IL: Waste Management and Research Center, 1985.

Felton, Paul Ellsworth. "The History of the Atlantic and Great Western Railroad." PhD diss. Pittsburg, PA: University of Pittsburgh, 1943.

Tri-Urban Directory of Hammond and East Chicago, Indiana, and Hegewisch, Illinois . . . for 1889–1890. Hammond, IN: Frank E. Gero, 1889. Reprint edition. Hammond, IN: Hammond Historical Society, 1976.

Forney, Matthias N. *The Railroad Car Builders Pictorial Dictionary.* Toronto or London: Dover Publications Inc., 1974.

Gates, Grace Hooten. *The Model City of the New South, Anniston, Alabama, 1872–1900.* Tuscaloosa: University of Alabama Press, 1978.

Pittenger, E. and S. Franiak, eds. *[John Harris's] Hegewisch in a Nutshell.* Pamphlet. 1936.

Hegewisch, Eddie. Online correspondence, February–March 2015 for Adolf Hegewisch.

Hegewisch News, Hegewisch News Weekly, and the *News Weekly.* April 1936–September 1990.

Interviews with Hegewisch residents and oral history tapes from Southeast Chicago Historical Museum collection

Lake Calumet Airport collection at Southeast Chicago Historical Museum

Landing, James E. "Conceptual Plan for the Lake Calumet Ecological Park: Chicago, Illinois." 1986.

New York Public Library online research department

White, John H., Jr. *The American Railroad Freight Car: From the Wood-car Era to the Coming of Steel.* Baltimore, MD: The Johns Hopkins University Press, 1993.

Discover Thousands of Local History Books Featuring Millions of Vintage Images

Arcadia Publishing, the leading local history publisher in the United States, is committed to making history accessible and meaningful through publishing books that celebrate and preserve the heritage of America's people and places.

Find more books like this at
www.arcadiapublishing.com

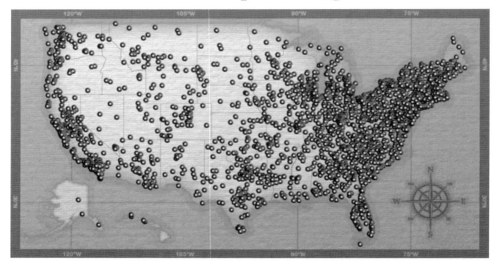

Search for your hometown history, your old stomping grounds, and even your favorite sports team.

Consistent with our mission to preserve history on a local level, this book was printed in South Carolina on American-made paper and manufactured entirely in the United States. Products carrying the accredited Forest Stewardship Council (FSC) label are printed on 100 percent FSC-certified paper.

MADE IN THE USA